THE SECRETS OF ALKAZAR

A Book of Magic

by Allan Zola Kronzek
illustrations by Tom Huffman

Four Winds Press   New York

LIBRARY OF CONGRESS CATALOGING IN PUBLICATION DATA

Kronzek, Allan Z
  The secrets of Alkazar.

  1. Conjuring. I. Title.
GV1547.K76   793.8   80-11436
ISBN 0-590-07425-3

PUBLISHED BY FOUR WINDS PRESS
A DIVISION OF SCHOLASTIC MAGAZINES, INC., NEW YORK, N.Y.
TEXT COPYRIGHT © 1980 BY ALLAN ZOLA KRONZEK
ILLUSTRATIONS COPYRIGHT © 1980 BY TOM HUFFMAN
ALL RIGHTS RESERVED
PRINTED IN THE UNITED STATES OF AMERICA
LIBRARY OF CONGRESS CATALOG CARD NUMBER: 80-11436
1   2   3   4   5   84   83   82   81   80

To Sarah Shapira

Acknowledgments

For awakening and fostering my interest in magic, I wish to thank my parents, Fannie and Saul Kronzek. My sister, Diane, deserves belated praise for her services as my first assistant, and my daughter, Edith, has been wonderfully helpful as an audience and critic.

Most of all, I am deeply indebted to my wife, Bibi Wein Kronzek, for her invaluable work on the manuscript, editorial advice, typing, love, understanding, and support.

My thanks also to Maria Polushkin Robbins for initiating this project, and to Beverly Reingold for helping me conclude it. And for owning the local magic store and being there for so many young magicians, a special thanks to Jim Swoger.

Contents

Preface **1**

1 MISDIRECTION: Passing Through **2**

2 THE HANDLING: Sweet Deception **10**

3 SECRETS: The Stamp Collector **18**

4 PRESENTATION: The Cords of Shastri **26**

5 PATTER: Cut and Restored Rope **36**

6 REPETITION: Homing Stones **48**

7 CARDS, PART ONE: Magnetic Touch **56**

8 CARDS, PART TWO: Super Ears **66**

9 CARDS, PART THREE: The Speller The Assistant
The Mirror ESP **76**

10 NATURALNESS: Coins Through the Table **88**

11 ROUTINING: Card in Orange **100**

12 PERFORMANCE: The Spirit of Isis **112**

Afterword **121**

Preface

People have always been fascinated by magic. It fills the pages of our folk and fairy tales and is one of the first things we learn about as children. Because it deals with supernatural forces, magic is also a religious idea. It is Zeus's thunderbolts, the miracles of the prophets, and the practices of witch doctors, shamen, and medicine men. In the broadest sense, magic is a force so powerful it can overturn the laws of nature and cause impossible events to happen. But to draw upon this force, one must possess the secrets.

The secrets of Alkazar, of course, are nothing but tricks. Unlike the power of legendary magic, magic as entertainment is all fraud and deception. The magician is a swindler, a liar, and a cheat. What he offers is not true magic but mere illusion based on the tricks of the theater and the confidence man. And yet, at his best, the skilled magician can show us things so astonishing, so utterly impossible and without explanation that our senses reel, and for a brief moment the trick we're watching becomes real magic.

For my general approach to this subject, I am deeply indebted to Alkazar, with whom I studied as a boy and whom I still see now and then, when my magician's claws need sharpening. Throughout the years his encouragement and criticism have been invaluable. I am also grateful for his permission to use so much material from his Red and Black Notebooks. These observations on the theory and practice of magic were written for his students and were never intended for publication. Most of all, I am indebted to him for the dedication and spirit with which he approached his art. It was Alkazar who taught me that tricks need not always be tricks. They can also be magic.

1

MISDIRECTION

passing through

Much of your success as a magician will depend on your ability to perform certain actions in full view of the audience, without anyone becoming aware of what you are doing. This is not accomplished by being secretive or quick with your hands. In fact, quick movements are among the easiest to detect. Rather, it is done by cleverly directing the attention of the viewers away from the secret action and toward something else. This is called *misdirection*. It is one of the most powerful and important tools a magician has. By understanding how it works and how to use it, you can influence not only what the audience sees, but also what they believe.

When I first began my studies with Alkazar, he gave me a set of principles concerning misdirection. They are excellent observations and apply to nearly all the magic I have ever done.

THE PRINCIPLES OF MISDIRECTION

The key to misdirection lies in learning to control attention.

PRINCIPLE I

The audience will pay attention to what moves. They will also pay attention to what makes noise.

What doesn't move and doesn't make noise doesn't attract attention.

PRINCIPLE II

The audience will always look where the magician looks.

The magician must never look at what he wishes to conceal.

PRINCIPLE III

The audience will treat as important what the magician treats as important.

The audience will treat as unimportant what the magician treats as unimportant.

The magician nearly always treats what is important as if it were unimportant. Likewise, he treats what is unimportant as if it were important.

Now, let's look at some of these ideas at work. The following trick is an ideal place to begin because the misdirection is built right into it. It is easily done on the spur of the moment and is one of Alkazar's favorites. He calls it *Passing Through*.

While seated around the dinner table or at a restaurant with friends, Alkazar announces that he is going to perform a miracle. He is going to cause a coin to pass through the table. He borrows a quarter and places it on the table. Next, he covers some handy object—a salt shaker, for instance —with a napkin and places it on top of the coin.

5

Alkazar places one hand under the table to receive the coin. He utters some magic words and orders the coin to pass through the table. He then lifts the shaker to show that the quarter is gone. To the wizard's surprise, nothing has happened. The coin is still there.

But wait. Alkazar suddenly notices that the coin is heads up instead of tails up. No wonder it didn't work. The magician turns the quarter over, covers it with the salt shaker, and again utters some magic words. But once again, the magic fails.

By this time the audience is beginning to wonder. Is Alkazar really a magician? Of course he is—and now he proves it. "There is a very powerful spell I don't use often, because it can be dangerous," he announces. "But this is no time to be cautious."

Again he covers the coin with the salt shaker. "Atoms and molecules," chants the mystifier, "by the power that is mine, I order you to make way. Oomash Kavasi Zid!" Without warning, Alkazar slams his hand down on the napkin and, instantaneously, the salt shaker passes through the table and is immediately brought up from underneath! What has taken place is an impossible demonstration of one solid object passing through another. As for the quarter, it is still lying on the table under the now-crumpled napkin. Alkazar returns it to its owner with a smile and says, "Sometimes the powers of magic surprise even me." He then begins another feat of mystery.

What makes this trick so stunning in Alkazar's hands is not merely the secret, but the way in which he uses misdirection and surprise to throw the audience off guard. Here's how to do it.

Place the borrowed coin on the table a foot or so in front of you. Take the salt shaker and cover it with the napkin, explaining that the penetration of the coin must take place out of sight. Squeeze and mold the napkin around the top and sides of the shaker so that the shape of the shaker is clear. Make sure the napkin hides the entire shaker, especially at the bottom, where the napkin spreads out onto the table. (See Figure 1-1.) Then take the napkin-shaker combination and place it on top of the coin.

Place your left hand under the table to receive the coin. Your right hand should hover a few inches above the shaker. Make a magical pass, commanding the coin to penetrate the table. Pause. Appear somewhat puzzled, and bring your left hand up from under the table. With your right hand, lift the shaker-napkin by grasping it near the very top between your thumb and middle finger, and bring it toward you so that it ends up slightly past the edge of the table and an inch or so above it. What you are supposedly doing is showing that the coin is still there, so make sure you look at the coin and pay no attention at all to your right hand. Glance at the spectators, and then "realize" that the coin is wrong side up. Lean forward just a bit, and with your left hand turn the coin over. At the exact time that you are turning the coin, lower your right hand slightly so that the napkin touches the tabletop, loosen your grip, and allow the shaker to slip out of the napkin and fall into your lap. (See Figure 1-2.) Watch only the coin. Then take the napkin, which has kept the shape of the shaker (magicians call a hollow form like this a *shell*), and place it back over the coin as if the shaker were still inside. Release the napkin.

As bold as this move is, absolutely no one will realize what has just gone on because of the superb misdirection. From the very start, the audience has been led to believe that they are watching a coin trick. This causes them to think the napkin and the shaker are unimportant (Principle 3). The turning of the coin holds the audience's attention at the very moment the shaker is being "stolen" (Principles 1, 2, and 3). And, finally, the replacing of the shell causes the spectators to assume that the shaker is still there.

Continue by attempting once more to pass the coin through the table. This time, when you lift the "shaker" to show the coin, don't move it far from the coin. Then cover the coin again. To conclude the trick, say a few words about the very powerful magic you must use. As your left hand goes under the table, secretly pick up the salt shaker from your lap and hold it under the table, directly under the shell. Do this by touch alone. Under no

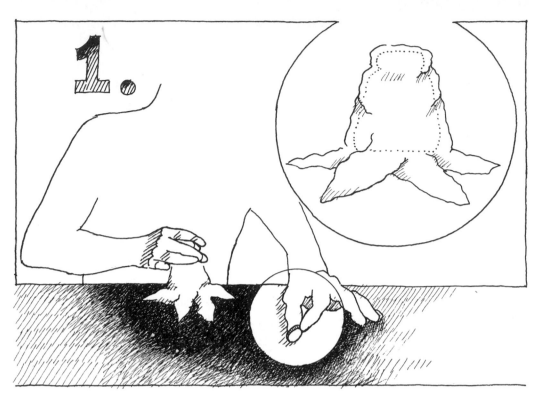

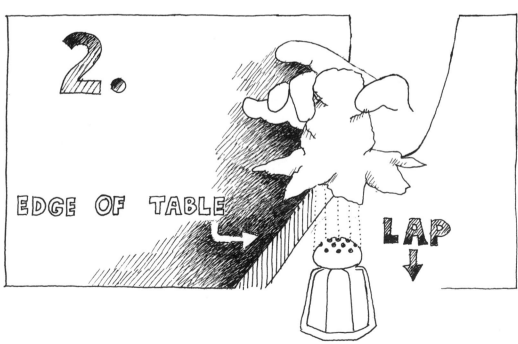

EDGE OF TABLE

LAP

circumstances should you look at your left hand or the shaker. Slam your open right hand down onto the shell and smash it flat against the table. Immediately bring the shaker up for all to see. The illusion of passing through is perfect.

Here are eight important tips on this trick from Alkazar's *Black Notebook:*

1. Just as you must make the coin seem important to the trick, you must make the salt shaker seem unimportant.
2. Always handle the shell as if it really contained the shaker.
3. Learn what kinds of napkins will hold a shape. Stiff paper napkins are ideal. Newspaper is an excellent substitute.
4. Never lift the shell so high or tilt it at such an angle that the audience will be able to see inside.
5. Never rush through the coin part of the trick. Act as if you genuinely expect the coin to penetrate the table.
6. Keep the shell even with or slightly below the edge of the table when you release the shaker. If you do so, the maneuver will be impossible to detect.
7. Work on the timing of the coin turn and the shaker drop, so that you do them simultaneously and without hesitating or fumbling.
8. Add or subtract from the trick whatever makes it work best for you. Many magicians steal the shaker on the second peek. It's a matter of choice.

2

THE HANDLING

sweet deception

One rule about performing magic is so simple and obvious I'm not sure I should even mention it. But I'm going to anyway, because, like so many obvious things, it is easily overlooked. It's this: In order to create magic, you must know what you are doing.

That's it. That's the whole thing. But knowing what you are doing means more than knowing the secret of any particular trick. Anyone can know a secret. What a magician must know is a total performance. You must know how to introduce a trick, how to build interest in it, how to handle props, how to direct or misdirect attention, and generally how to do the dozen or so things necessary to turn tricks into magic.

So how do you begin to know a trick? The first thing you must do is read the description of the effect. *Effect* is magicians' jargon for what appears to happen, or what the audience sees. Be sure to read the directions through a few times, to get the general idea of how the effect is produced. Next, with the necessary props in front of you, go through all the steps, or "moves," necessary to create the effect. Learn the order of the steps so thoroughly that you will never forget what comes next. Then go through all the steps again, this time paying very close attention to every detail.

In rehearsing a trick like Passing Through, you must know exactly how you should hold the napkin-shaker, where you are going to move it, and when you are going to let it go. Magicians call the way they approach these details the *handling* of the trick. Different handlings can be used to produce the same effect, and you must develop and learn yours so that you can do it exactly the same way every time, without thinking. You will have plenty of other things to occupy you during a performance, so the handling should be completely second nature.

When deciding your approach, consider the ways in which you can build misdirection into the handling. Also, try speeding up or slowing down various parts of the performance to see which tempos work best.

Practice each step of the trick separately, then work on the trick as a whole. Try to make everything flow. Practice until it stops being fun, take a rest, then practice some more.

Once you are satisfied that your rehearsals have given you something worth showing, take the trick out in public and polish it. Don't expect it to go perfectly at first. It probably won't. But keep at it. It is only by showing the same effect to different audiences that you can (1) learn how long it should be, (2) get the timing of each part right, (3) find and eliminate the dull spots, (4) overcome your nervousness, and, most important, (5) realize how something so simple can fool so many intelligent people.

Only when you have done all of this will you really know what you're doing when you present a trick. And then you will be unshakable. Your performance will seem spontaneous and unrehearsed. And you will be a magician.

Now try adding *Sweet Deception* to your repertoire. Alkazar often presents it as a follow-up to Passing Through. Done well, it's a knockout.

After returning the quarter to its owner, Alkazar explains that he doesn't use such powerful magic words often, because sometimes they summon spirits from another dimension, and these spirits can take days to go away. In fact, the magician remarks, the spirits are present at this very moment. The spectators seem doubtful, but Alkazar offers to prove it.

Noticing a bowl of sugar cubes on the table, the performer asks someone to pick out a cube and unwrap it. "I want you to think of a geometrical figure," the magician states. "It can be a circle, a square, a star, anything. When you have it pictured clearly in your mind, draw it on the cube."

Alkazar offers the volunteer a dark lead pencil. After the figure has been drawn, he takes the cube, and, without looking at the design, drops it into a glass of water, where it begins to dissolve.

"Now, please hold your hand above the glass," the magician says. "You'll probably feel a tingling sensation in a moment, but try not to move. May we have absolute quiet."

During the silence, Alkazar moves his hands mysteriously around the glass but never once touches it.

"Spirits," he finally says, "we have drawn for you; now draw for us!"

The conjuror claps his hands, or whispers a half-heard chant.

"Please turn your hand palm up so that we may all see."

The volunteer does so, and there on his palm the audience sees the exact same shape that he drew on the sugar cube!

As with most tricks, the secret of the effect is quite simple. But, as most magicians know, the simplest of things are often the most difficult to detect. Here are the basic moves.

1. While the volunteer is drawing on the cube, secretly wet the ball of your right thumb. You could openly lick your thumb and probably no one would notice. It's easier, though, simply to move the glass of water to the center of the table, and at the same time allow your thumb to get wet by touching the inside rim.

2. Have the volunteer give you the cube, or place it drawing-side down on the table. Take it between the thumb and forefinger of your hand, and drop it into the water without looking at the design. (See Figure 2-1.) While doing so, secretly press your thumb (the moist one) against the drawing, and, after dropping the cube, keep your thumb hidden under your

fingers as you withdraw your hand. The reason for hiding your thumb is that it now bears the imprint of the drawing that is on the cube.

3. Ask the volunteer to hold his hand over the glass. Pretend it's very important for him to hold his hand in exactly the right place, and ask him to raise it an inch, then lower it half an inch. Pretending he still doesn't have it right, reach over, take his hand, and raise or lower it. As you do this, briefly press your thumb against his palm, transferring the drawing. (See Figure 2-2.) Say something like, "Now hold it right there," and withdraw your hand, again keeping your thumb with the imprint out of sight.

4. As you ask for silence and give your final instructions, lower your right hand beneath the table and quickly wipe the lead smudge from your thumb. Finally, bring both hands forward, make some magical passes (to show how free of trickery your hands are) and complete the effect.

I have a few splendid tips from Alkazar, but first let me suggest you work on some of the things that will help you know this trick. How and when are you going to wet your thumb? Where will the spectators' attention be while you are doing this? What handling are you going to use to pick up the cube? And, most important of all, do you know this trick well enough to perform it without thinking?

From the *Black Notebook:*

1. When you tell the volunteer how to hold his hand, he will generally ask, "Like this?" At that moment, take his hand, move it slightly up or down as you transfer the imprint, and say, "No, like this."

2. Once the imprint has been transferred, tell the volunteer to make a tight fist. This makes the revealing of the drawing more dramatic.

3. After the transfer, when the volunteer's hand is in place above the glass, ask him if he feels a tingling sensation. This puts additional time between

15

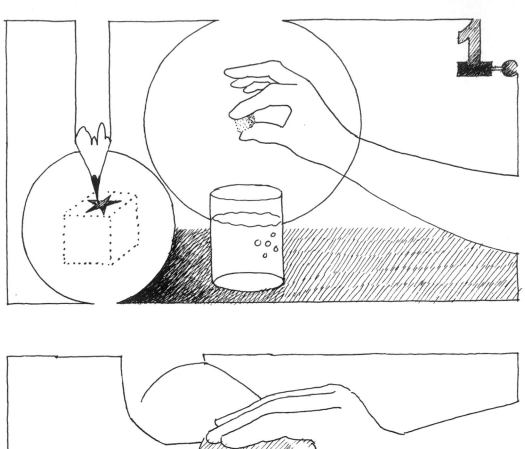

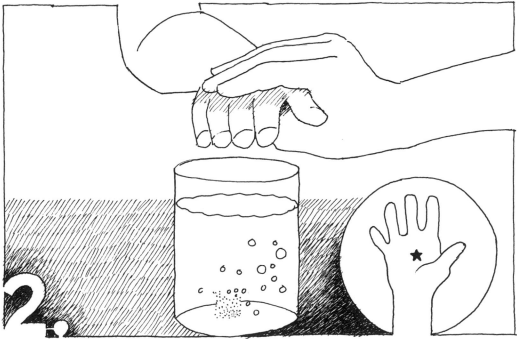

the transferring and the revealing, during which the volunteer often forgets that you ever touched his hand.

4. When doing magic with common objects such as salt shakers, sugar cubes, napkins, or pieces of paper, always make it seem as if you are using these things simply because they are handy. Any others, it should seem, would do just as well.

5. *An alternate performance:* With an audience of seven or eight, when the mood is right, present Sweet Deception as a seance. One person draws the figure but shows it to no one. The magician drops the cube into the glass. A different spectator places his hand above the glass and makes a fist. Everyone else joins hands. The first person announces what he drew. Everyone concentrates on it. The fist is opened and the drawing revealed. Fantastic!

3

SECRETS

the stamp collector

"Hey, how did you do that?"

Everyone asks. Friends, teachers, parents, visitors from out of town—they all want to know how it's done. Say, "It's magic," change the subject, or continue your performance. But whatever you do, don't tell.

Protecting the secrets of magic has always been one of the sacred duties of every serious magician. Magicians tell other magicians and set their ideas down in books. But no magician ever reveals the *modus operandi* (the way an effect works) simply to satisfy the curiosity of a spectator.

There are several reasons for this. First, the more the public knows about the devices of magic, the more difficult it becomes to use these devices successfully. Second, revealing the secret diminishes the audience's appreciation of the magician's craft. Audiences assume that "the secret" is the essence of the magician's art. Even a few magicians believe this. However, as Alkazar taught me, it is always the performance, never the secret, that determines great magic.

But perhaps the worst thing about exposing the secret is that it denies the audience enjoyment. So much of what is pleasurable about watching magic is the astonishment that comes from not understanding how it is created. When you reveal your methods, you burst the audience's magical

20

balloon. Out go the mystery, the wonder, and the sense of the impossible. And instead of a baffled spectator, you have a disappointed one.

Devices like hidden threads and trap doors, are, of course, of endless fascination to magicians. But they are the tools of magic and should remain strictly backstage. As Alkazar puts it, "The entertainment of magic springs from effects, not causes."

The following effect is created from two of magic's most ingenious devices, the *shortened edge* and the *secret pocket*. Both devices can be used to create a number of startling effects. This one is called *The Stamp Collector*.

In the midst of his performance, the magician notices that he has "accidentally" brought with him a drinking glass filled with loose postage stamps. Stamp collecting is his hobby, he explains to the audience, and he had meant to paste the stamps in his stamp album the previous night. However, if no one objects, he will tend to the job right now with the aid of magic.

The magician leafs through a stamp album to show that all the pages are blank. He gives the album to a member of the audience who has come on-stage to assist him. Next, the magician shows a square of newspaper, which he folds into a cone. He pours the stamps from the glass into the cone.

The magician stands on one side of the stage, holding the cone at arm's length. The spectator stands at the opposite end of the stage and holds the album, with two hands, above his head.

"By the powers that are mine," the magician intones, "I order you to fly!"

With a snap of his finger and a flourish of his hand, the wizard strikes the cone and flips it open. The stamps are gone! The performer takes the album from the spectator and flips through the pages again. The album is now completely filled with stamps.

To perform The Stamp Collector, you need to make two devices, a cone for vanishing the stamps and an album that can be shown empty or filled, whichever you choose.

21

The album should be an ordinary dime-store scrapbook, which you can buy for two or three dollars. Don't buy a stamp album; buy a scrapbook, preferably the binder type from which the paper can be removed. Remove the paper and divide it into two equal piles. Using scissors or a single-edged razor blade, carefully trim a 1/8-inch strip off the right side of every page in one of the piles. This is best done by placing a ruler or yardstick near the edge of the paper and slicing down against it, or by drawing a line and then cutting with scissors. The 1/8-inch measurement doesn't have to be exact, but it should be close.

Next, combine the two piles by placing a shortened page between every regular page so that you end up with a stack of regular and shortened pages alternating throughout. Place this setup back into the binder. If you can't get a scrapbook with removable pages, you can do the trimming with the pages still in, cutting every other page, beginning with the second page.

Now, lay the album on a table in front of you. Open the cover and turn the first page over. On the two pages in front of you, paste several rows of stamps. Then turn to the next two pages, but don't paste down any stamps. Turn to the next pair and paste stamps. Go through the entire album in this way, so that one pair of facing pages will have stamps, the next won't, and so on. The first and last pages of the album should not have stamps.

You will now find that, depending upon which direction you flip through the album, the stamps will or will not show. If you grasp all the pages between your left thumb and fingers and let them flip off your left thumb, front to back, only the blank pages will show. This is how you show the album the first time. The second time, using your right hand, flip the pages from back to front. Only the pages with stamps will show. (See Figure 3-1.) This is the result of the shortened pages, which cause two pages to fall together as if they were one.

The vanishing of the stamps is accomplished via a secret compartment in the paper that is used to form the cone. To prepare the paper, cut out two squares of newspaper, 7 or 8 inches on every side. Spread a thin layer of glue around three sides of one square and glue it to the other square. When the glue is dry, trim the three glued sides with scissors so that the papers don't overlap. It should look like a single piece of paper. (It's a good idea to make up several sets of papers at the same time and save them for future use.)

To vanish the stamps during a performance, pick up the newspaper from your table, show it casually, and fold it into a cone. To do this, hold the paper in your right hand with the opening on the left side. Bring the lower left corner to "X" and crease the paper along that line. Bring the upper right corner to "Y" and crease again. Then fold the tail up to prevent anything from falling out. (See Figure 3-2.)

Hold the cone in your left hand and spread the mouth open by placing the fingers of the right hand inside and pushing out the sides. While doing this, open the secret compartment as wide as it will go. Pour the stamps into the compartment and then press the cone flat. To show that the stamps have disappeared, simply unfold the cone, or take it between your right thumb and forefinger at the point where the stamps went in and shake it open with a snap. Show both sides of the paper, and if you're not concerned about the stamps, crumple the paper and toss it aside.

That's all the technical information you need to produce the effect. But there's still a lot to be done. So far, all you know is the main secret, and that alone will get you nowhere. You must now develop an exact and deceptive handling, and create a performance in which you will seem to be doing magic, not operating mechanical devices.

And now, some observations by Alkazar. First, from the *Black Notebook:*

1. When you order the stamps to vanish, follow them with your eyes as they fly invisibly through the air and enter the album.
2. Draw a small x on the newspaper to mark the open side. You will be able to handle the paper more freely if you know which side is which. No one in the audience will be the wiser.

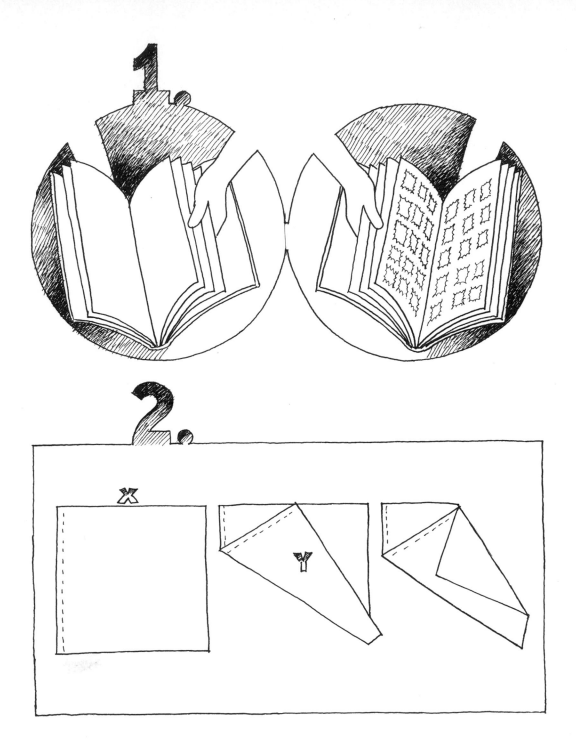

3. When you give the album to the volunteer, tell him to grasp it tightly so that nothing can get in or out. This will prevent him from examining the album while the stamps are being vanished.

And from the *Red Notebook:*

1. A magic secret is any hidden principle, method, or device used to create a magical effect.
2. The quickest way to erase the pleasure of seeing magic is to tell the audience how it's done.
3. Never blame those who discover your secrets. The fault is always the magician's.

CHAPTER

4

PRESENTATION

the cords of shastri

Most presentations—ways of showing a trick—are built around a central story or idea called a *theme*. A theme provides a specific way of presenting an effect from beginning to end. It gives the magician interesting things to talk about and increases the opportunities for drama, mystery, and surprise. And, most important, a theme makes an effect be "about" something.

There will probably be many times when the suggested theme for an effect will seem entirely out of keeping with the way you want to do magic. Alkazar's version of Passing Through, for example, is built around his claims of wizardry and supernatural powers. He is boastful, mysterious, and pompous, all of which suit his personality. Yet you may feel ridiculous carrying on in this fashion. In order to perform Passing Through and feel comfortable doing it, you may need a very different version of the trick. Perhaps something like this:

28

The performer, seated at a table with friends, is asked to do some magic.

"Magic?" he replies. "There is no such thing. Don't you know that magic tricks are actually based on little-known scientific facts? Salt melts ice. Everyone knows that. But not everyone knows that under certain conditions salt can also melt wood, plastic, and many other materials."

To prove his claim, the magician sprinkles some salt on the table, borrows a quarter, and places it on the salt. The salt shaker is then placed on top of the coin "to add a little weight," and the whole thing is covered with a napkin "because it works better in the dark."

The performer places his hand under the table and waits for the coin to fall through. Twice the magician lifts the shaker to check on the progress of the coin, but it hasn't moved at all.

"I know this works," the magician insists. "Maybe all it needs is a little push." And with that he slaps his hand down on the napkin—and the entire shaker falls through the table.

The handling and basic effect of Passing Through have not changed at all, yet what the trick is "about" is now entirely different. A new theme—the little-known power of salt—has shifted the reason for the effect from a demonstration of the magician's powers to a "scientific" demonstration. It may not be a wizard's version of Passing Through, but for the performer who wants to act more like himself, it is ideal.

With a little imagination, you should have no trouble coming up with many good themes. One approach is to start with the basic effect in mind, and try to think up theories or little-known "facts" that purport to explain how the effect is created. First state the theory to your audience, then perform the effect to prove that the theory is true.

Another approach might be to build a presentation around some ordinary object. The theme of Sweet Deception, for example, is "the presence of spirits." But it might just as well be "the magic pencil." You can explain where the pencil came from, how it got its power, and how you happen to own it. Then show how it works.

History, mythology, and current events are excellent places to search for new themes. Almost any theme can work if you convincingly relate it to the effect you're performing. What matters is that the presentation you come up with feel comfortable to perform and be appropriate to your audience.

The following effect uses a secret method known to magicians for over four hundred years. This presentation—one of many possible—is based on the theme of "magic ropes." It was created by Alkazar especially for young audiences. He calls it *The Cords of Shastri.*

"Boys and girls," begins the famous magician, "for centuries wizards the world over have been searching in vain for the lost Cords of Shastri—two ropes said to have the power to pass through any substance without harming it. Some have said the cords are just a legend—that they never existed. But I believe that everything said about the cords is absolutely true! And if two people from the audience will come up and help me, I'll show you why."

Two volunteers are chosen from the audience. As they make their way forward, Alkazar displays a long narrow box from which he carefully removes two long red ropes.

"These were discovered in India only a few days ago, and have just been sent to me for testing. If they are indeed the Cords of Shastri, we are about to witness a feat of magic that hasn't been seen on this earth for two thousand years!"

Alkazar gives one of the volunteers (known as the "victim") a pair of metal rings, telling him to hold one in each hand. Then, standing behind the victim, Alkazar threads the magic ropes through the rings. He gives one set of rope ends to the second assistant, and holds one set himself.

"On the count of three," Alkazar explains, "we'll pull on the cords. If the legend is true, they'll pass right through these solid steel rings without harm to either the ropes or the rings. Watch!

"One . . . two . . . thr— No! Wait! Stop everything!"

Alkazar stares at the cords in disbelief. He seems terribly worried. He looks at the cords, then at the audience, then again at the cords.

"Do you realize," he finally says to the victim, "that if this works the cords are going to slice right through your body? Have you ever done this before?"

"No," the victim replies fearfully.

"Neither have I," says Alkazar, "but this is no time to worry. In fact, let's make it even harder."

Alkazar takes one of the helper's ropes, crosses it with one of his own, and ties an overhand knot, thus encasing the victim in a circle of rope. Again the countdown is made, and this time the impossible happens. The ropes are pulled, and instantaneously they not only pass through the rings, they appear to penetrate the victim's body, ending up stretched out in front of him.

Alkazar thanks the volunteers for their help, and they return to their seats amid a round of applause.

To create this fine illusion, you need two rings, two cords or ropes, each about 8 feet long, and a small length of thread. It doesn't matter what you use for cords. I prefer thick, colored yarn. Alkazar uses soft, silken rope dyed red or blue. Ribbon also works well. The rings can be curtain rings, embroidery hoops, or even short cardboard tubes cut from the core of a roll of paper towels and decorated.

To prepare for a performance, fold each of the cords in half. Place the two middles back to back, and tie the cords together at that point with the thread. Now make a loose fist around the prepared middle portion, and it will appear that you are holding two separate pieces of rope that run end to end through your fist. (See Figure 4-1.) This is the key deception: What the audience assumes are the ends of different ropes are actually the ends of the same rope. Before your performance, lay the cords on your table so that the prepared part, or *gimmick,* is hidden from view, or, like Alkazar, place the cords in a long florist's box.

Here are the basic moves. During your opening remarks, pick up the ropes (always with a loose fist around the joined centers) and display them to the audience. With your free hand, take hold of the ropes near one set of ends (your other hand should still cover the centers) and snap the ropes between your hands to demonstrate their strength. When the assistants arrive onstage, decide which will be the victim and hand him the rings. If you need to put the ropes down while getting the rings, make sure the gimmick remains out of view.

Holding the joined centers in your left hand, move to a position behind the victim. With your right hand, thread the right pair of ends through the ring in the victim's right hand. Have the assistant take the ends and back away until most of the slack is taken up. Meanwhile, bring your left hand directly behind and close to the victim's back. Change your grip on the ropes so you can thread the left ends through the remaining ring, and take a position opposite the assistant. Make sure to keep enough tension on the ropes so that the gimmick remains securely in place behind the victim's back. You now have the arrangement seen in Figure 4-2. A view from behind the victim is shown in Figure 4-3.

Since you are still holding both ends of the same rope, it is now necessary to exchange one of your ends for one of the assistant's. That's the purpose of tying the knot. Not only does it switch the ropes, it also makes everything appear more difficult.

To tie the knot, take one of the helper's cords in your free (left) hand and flip one of your cords across it so that it hangs down. Transfer the rope in your right hand to your left, and with your right hand reach down through the V formed by the cords, take the end of the dangling rope, pull it up through the V, and hand it to the assistant. You still hold one of the assistant's cords, so that you have now exchanged ropes. Move back to your original position, and gently tighten the knot. The final position is shown in Figure 4-4.

All that remains is to build the effect to an exciting climax and pull on the cords. The pull—which should be forward and toward yourself—will

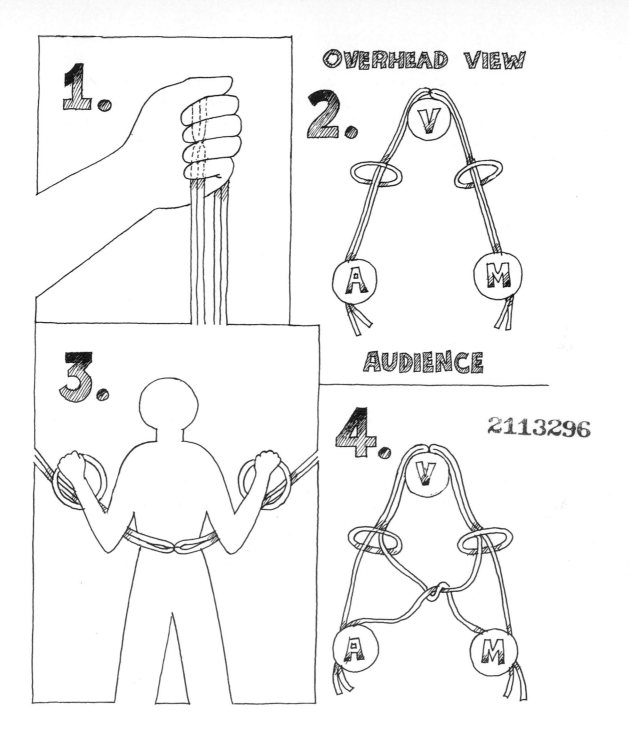

break the thread, allowing the ropes to zip around the victim's waist and through the centers of the rings. It all happens so fast that the illusion of the ropes passing through the body is amazingly convincing. You might even fool yourself.

As you can imagine, Alkazar's theme of magic cords works marvelously well for young audiences. They often believe the story completely, and the magician's doubts about the outcome create a sense of danger that makes the presentation highly dramatic. An older audience, however, won't buy the story for a minute, and you might feel uncomfortable trying to pass it off as true.

See what presentations you can come up with for older audiences, based on some of the ideas in Alkazar's *Black Notebook*. Developing the right presentation for yourself and your audience is one of the most creative and enjoyable parts of a magician's homework. And The Cords of Shastri, a truly splendid illusion, deserves the best presentation you can give it.

From the *Black Notebook*:

1. Handle the ropes loosely. A tight fist is not needed to hide the gimmick and will only call attention to itself.
2. Use thread that is neither so weak that it breaks too soon, nor so strong that it doesn't break at all.
3. Tie the overhand knot as an afterthought. It is one of the keys to the effect, so the less attention paid to it, the better.
4. Build the illusion into something daring and unusual. Tell the audience they will actually see the cords penetrate the assistant's body. When it's over, many will believe they saw just that.
5. *Alternate themes:*
   A. Present a new invention (the rings can be antennae that collect mysterious rays from outer space) that the volunteer wears and that "alters the molecular structure of the body so that solid objects may pass through it."
   B. Eliminate the rings—the effect works as well without them—

presenting a new version of the classic sawing-in-half illusion with a comic twist. "I wanted to saw somebody in half today," you begin, "but my mother wouldn't let me bring the saw—especially after what I did to the cat. So instead I brought these ropes, and . . ."

C. Try the theme of escape artistry (again without the rings). The great Houdini freed himself from ropes not by untying them, but by walking through them.

And from the *Red Notebook,* some tips on using assistants from the audience:

1. Always choose volunteers who are enjoying your performance. Never attempt to prove how clever you are by accepting the help of someone who pretends to know how everything is done.
2. Treat your assistants with respect. Most people enjoy being fooled. They do not enjoy feeling foolish.
3. If an assistant becomes fearful of what you are doing, whisper some words of reassurance. No one else will hear, and it will make the assistant more at ease.

5

PATTER

cut and restored rope

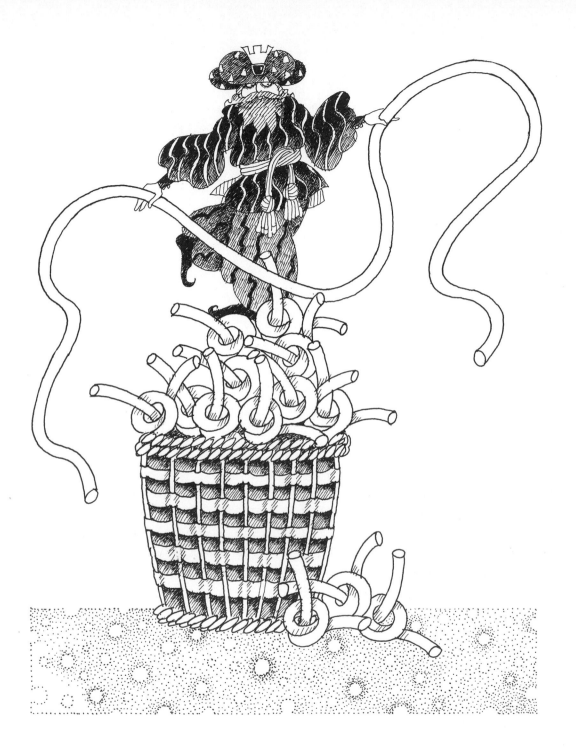

"Ladies and gentlemen," I began, "here I have an ordinary piece of string, which I'm about to cut in half and make whole again."

"Wrong!" interrupted Alkazar. "First, you're telling too much in advance. And second, that miserable piece of string is a piece of string—not an *ordinary* piece of string."

We were working on the subject of *patter,* which is the magician's word for the spoken part of a performance. In one sentence I had made two big mistakes.

"That's what comes from not preparing a script in advance," Alkazar chided me. "Sure, you can make up some of the patter as you go. We all do.

38

But not until you've thought out a complete script and made sure it works. That's the part of your homework you haven't done."

As Alkazar explained, systematic work on patter improves every part of a performance. It helps avoid blunders, improves the clarity of the theme, and forces the performer to coordinate words and actions in a way that eliminates weak points in the trick. Alkazar's method of developing patter is divided into three steps. They should be practiced after you have learned the handling of the effect and have chosen what seems like a good theme.

STEP I: DISCOVERY

Perform the effect exactly as you would before an audience, talking aloud and saying whatever comes into your head. Almost automatically, you'll begin to add details to the theme and discover new ways to present it. The theme will provide most of the subject matter of the patter, but don't leave out directions to spectators, or any comments you might ordinarily make. If you're rehearsing an effect to be shown close up, speak directly to imaginary individuals. Ask questions and make up replies. If you're preparing for a living-room or stage performance, speak as you would to a group.

At first you may sound awkward and be at a loss for words. There may be points at which you know you should be saying something, only nothing comes to mind. Don't worry about this now. Go through the trick again and again, always talking aloud. That's what gets the ideas flowing. When you come up with a line or phrase you really like, write it down for future use. Step I will be complete when you know the amount of patter you need, its general content, and roughly where it goes.

STEP II: REFINEMENT

Go through the trick again, as in Step I. Only this time, don't skate by all those places where you hesitate, fumble for words, or say something that makes no sense. Now is the time to solve the problems. If the expression of an idea is giving you trouble, go to a dictionary or a thesaurus and make sure you're using the right words. What's the point of what you are trying to say? How many different ways can you say it? How can you say it most clearly?

If you simply need more to say, do some research into the theme. You might try current events for ideas. Joke and humor books, indexed by subject, can sometimes furnish good lines—but don't use more than one or two.

If a problem can't be cleared up, the trouble might be in the theme, not the patter. In that case, find a new theme that you can work with.

If you have access to a tape recorder, tape yourself and analyze the way you sound. Step II will be complete when you can talk your way through a performance in a confident and relaxed manner, without hesitating or saying the wrong thing. You may use different words each time, but everything must be smooth and clear.

STEP III: COORDINATION

Scour the trick for dull spots—points where the pace slows down too much because of some necessary but time-consuming action. Create a line of patter that will move the trick forward, and always use it to fill a dull spot. A bit of information concerning the theme will usually do. So will a humorous aside or comment. Often the pace can be picked up simply by moving a line from elsewhere in the trick. The story of The Cords of Shastri, for example, could be used as the volunteers come onstage, instead of before.

Next, study the effect for points at which you're doing something tricky and are afraid of being caught. Find a line of patter to use as misdirection at these points. Again, it can be a fresh line or one taken from elsewhere. Practice the line with the secret action until they go together as a unit. Remember, it is not only the meaning of your words that act as misdirection, but also the fact that you are speaking to someone and thus focusing attention on that person. You'll find a sample script showing the coordination of patter and action at the end of this chapter.

It is up to you to choose how much patter to memorize and how much to make up on the spot. Improvised patter generally sounds more lively and spontaneous than a memorized script, and in close-up work it can encourage an effective interchange between magician and spectator. But memorized patter has the advantage of sounding sharp, and will help you to avoid the mistakes that can occur when improvising. Try both approaches or a combination. If you've followed Alkazar's three steps, you should be well prepared.

The following presentation is Alkazar's close-up version of the classic *Cut and Restored Rope.* In it, he uses the minimum of patter to achieve the maximum effect. It goes like this:

Several times during his show, Alkazar has checked his watch for the correct time. He does so again, then immediately removes from his pocket a pair of scissors, a long piece of string, and a small bottle filled with tiny knots of string. He places everything on the table and uncaps the bottle. He then picks up the string, cuts it in half, and ties the two pieces back together.

"It's important to cut it in the middle," he tells the audience. "That's how you get the best ones. Knots, I mean. I've been collecting them ever since I got this unusual piece of string. You see, if I cut it at exactly this time every day, I always get one fresh, juicy knot. And the amazing thing is, it's so easy to remove."

Suiting his actions to his words, Alkazar takes the knot between his thumb and forefinger and visibly slides it off the rope. The two pieces of string have suddenly become one again—as if they had never been cut. Alkazar adds the knot to those already in the bottle, puts the cap on, and returns the bottle, string, and scissors to his pocket.

41

The beauty of this trick is that it uses unprepared props and no mechanical devices of any kind, and can be done in several versions with nothing to set up in advance. It's all in the moves.

Begin with a piece of string or twine about 25 to 30 inches long. Display it between your hands. Then hold it in your left hand, as in Figure 5-1, so that about an inch of each end of the string is above your thumb, and the ends are about an inch apart. The middle of the string is located at point A.

With your right thumb and forefinger, grasp the string at point A and move your right hand upward toward your left hand. It appears to the audience that you are taking the center of the string in your right hand and placing it in your left hand, under your left thumb, in preparation for cutting. However, a switch takes place on the way up. As your right hand goes behind your left, where the audience can no longer see it, slip your thumb and forefinger under the loop you are lifting, as in Figure 5-2. Now place your thumb and forefinger together in a circle around point B of the leftmost string. Don't grip the string at point B; just make a circle around it. Continue the upward motion of your right hand. The original center of the string will automatically slip from your fingertips and another loop will come into view above your left hand. Briefly lift your left thumb and place this loop *between* the other two strings. Hold them all in place between your left thumb and forefinger, as in Figure 5-3. The audience will believe that this loop is the original center of the string. Actually, it is a piece near the end.

Although the moves have been described in steps, the lifting and placement of the loop in the left hand should appear to be one continuous motion, with no stops or hesitations when the switch takes place.

Pick up the scissors, cut the loop, and allow the four ends to be clearly seen, as in Figure 5-4. Just after cutting, release your hold on E and F and allow them to drop down. This move should be accomplished with a flick of the left wrist, an action that prevents the audience from seeing exactly which ends are being released, and also helps the string to fall into place. You now have the perfect illusion of two long and separate pieces of string. (See Figure 5-5.)

Next, tie an overhand knot in the short piece of string. The audience will think you are tying together the original center of the string. But actually you are tying C—D around the center of E—F. You'll need your left thumb and fingers to do this. You may use them freely, but make sure the gim-micked part of the string remains hidden from view until the knot is tight. If there is enough string left, tie a second knot on top of the first. Now hold the string from the ends and display the knot in the center. To all ap-pearances, you have simply cut the string and tied it back together at the same place.

To conclude the presentation given earlier, simply slide the knot off the string and place it in the bottle. However, if you are doing a standard Cut and Restored Rope, without the bottle and knot-collector theme, you may wish to conclude by causing the knot to vanish. To do this, hold one end of the rope between the thumb and forefinger of the left hand, and with the right hand, wind the rope around all four fingers of the left hand, which are cupped toward you. As you do, allow the rope to slide between the thumb and fingers of the right hand. When you come to the knot, hold it back in the right hand, but allow the rope to keep sliding through until all of it is wound around the left hand. Close your left hand. You now have the knot in your right hand and the restored rope around the left. The audience be-lieves the knot is somewhere in the left. To get rid of the knot, reach into your right pocket and remove a magic wand, a pencil, or some "invisibility dust," at the same time leaving the knot behind. Tap your left fist with the pencil, or sprinkle the dust. Finally, unwind the rope and show that it has been restored.

To show you how Alkazar has organized his patter for "The Knot Collec-tor," here is his presentation in script form:

ACTIONS	PATTER
Check time. Produce string, bottle, and scissors. Open bottle.	None.
Pick up string. Fold. Execute loop move. Hold loop in place for cutting.	None.

(Notice how the absence of patter works to help the effect. The loop move passes un-noticed because the audience has not been told what is going to happen and therefore has no idea what to look for. The silence and the props combine to arouse the spectators' curiosity and draw them into the trick.)

Pick up scissors. Cut rope. Let ends drop. Put down scissors.	"It's important to cut it in the middle. That's how you get the best ones.
Start tying knot.	"Knots, I mean. I've been collecting them ever since I got this unusual piece of string. You see, if I cut it—

(Note how the introduction of the theme at this point gives the magician plenty to say as he ties the knot.)

Finish tying knot and display rope.	"—at exactly this time every day, I always get one fresh, juicy knot. And the amazing thing is—
Take knot between thumb and forefinger of right hand. Slide knot from rope.	"—it's so easy to remove."
Pause until effect registers. Place knot in bottle and return props to pocket.	None.

44

And now, from the *Black Notebook:*

Alternate themes for Cut and Restored Rope:

1. "The Magic Lesson." Magician offers to teach the spectators the famous Cut and Restored Rope trick. Demonstrating as he goes, the magician explains that the cut rope is "restored" by means of a simple knot. Only most audiences fail to see the knot, owing to invisibility dust. The magician wraps the rope around his hand and sprinkles it with the magic dust. When the rope is unwound, the knot is invisible. The magician passes out free samples of the dust to each spectator and encourages them to try the trick when they get home.

2. "I once saw . . ." This presentation is based on the theme "I once saw a magician do a trick I've never been able to figure out." The magician successfully demonstrates the entire trick, all the while admiring the skill of the other magician and insisting on his own ignorance of how the effect is done. This theme can work with a variety of effects.

And from the *Red Notebook:*

The Do's and Don'ts of Patter

1. *Don't* expect to make it all up on the spot. Asking for inspiration is asking for trouble.
2. *Don't* copy anyone else's patter. Unless you're an actor, it won't sound natural. And it probably won't suit your age or performing style.
3. *Don't* tell the audience too much about what is going to happen. Saying "Write on this sugar cube and I'll make it appear on your hand" is pointing directly to the secret of the trick.
4. *Do* alert the audience when something special or unusual is about to happen. "Watch" is about as short and to the point as you can get.

5. *Don't* accompany your actions with a description of what the spectators can see for themselves. "Now I cut the string in half" is exactly what you shouldn't say when cutting a string in half.

6. *Do* address your remarks to individual spectators. Don't talk to the air.

7. *Don't* overtalk.

8. *Don't* use words like "ordinary" and "regular," as in "ordinary string." This suggests some string is not ordinary—and maybe this is it, after all.

9. *Do* say what you mean and mean what you say. Clarity and sincerity are the keys to good patter.

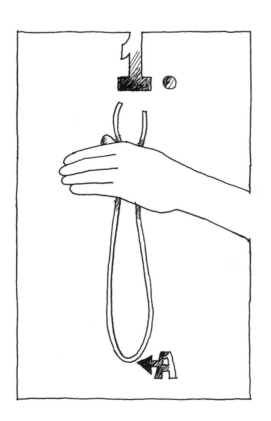
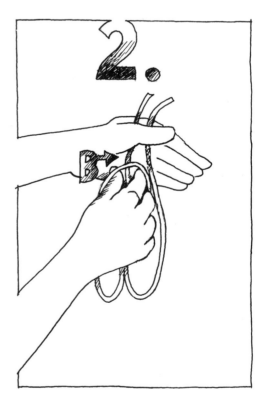

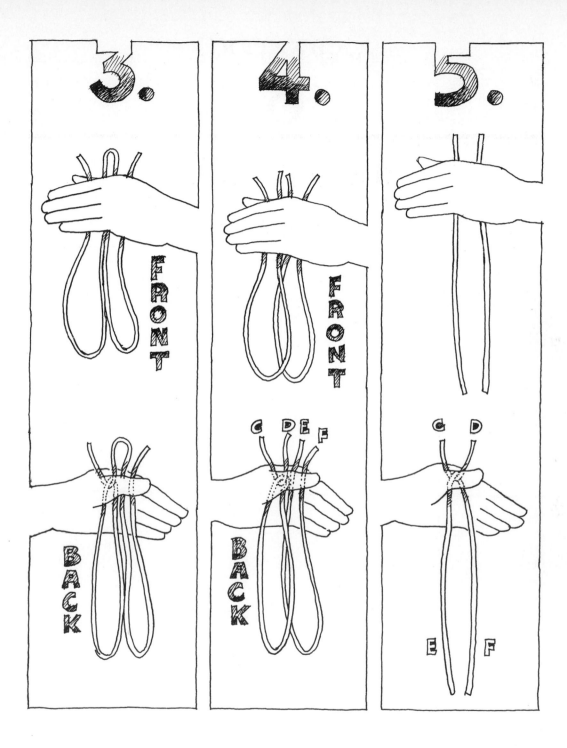

3.

FRONT

BACK

4.

FRONT

C D E F

BACK

5.

G D

E F

6

REPETITION

homing stones

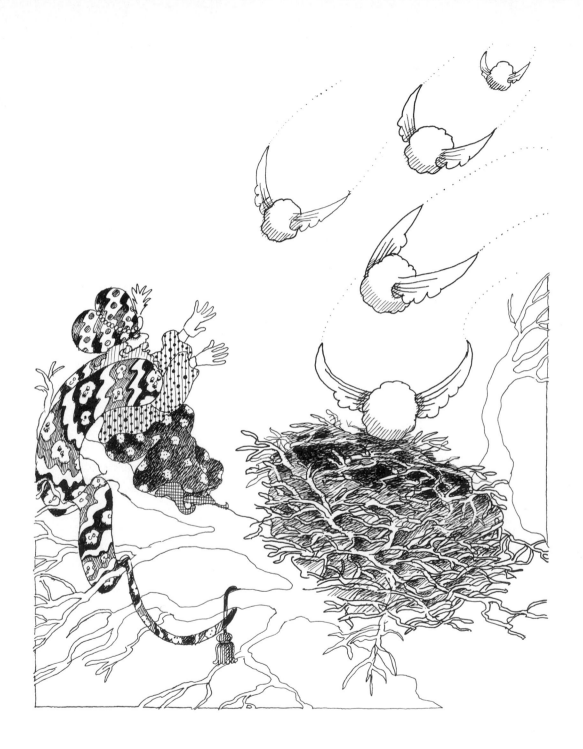

Occasionally, you will be asked to repeat a trick. Indeed, you may be mobbed by screaming fans who crowd around your kitchen table, congratulating you on what you've done and begging you to do it again. But beware! Resist! Stand firm. *Don't do it again.*

Why not? Because, first of all, it will never be the same. A repeated trick has been robbed of its surprise. Have you noticed how much of the magic in this book contains little twists that are unexpected? When the unexpected happens, the audience feels surprised, and this emotional surge is an important part of what makes a magic performance seem magical. "Never serve flat soda to your guests," says Alkazar, meaning that magic without the sparkle of surprise is not magic at all.

Which brings us to the next point. If it isn't magic, then what is it? The answer is, it's a puzzle. Remember that fellow who wants so much to see it again? Do you really think he wants a repeat performance so he can enjoy the magic a second time? He doesn't. What he really wants to do is solve the puzzle. He wants to reveal your secret and prove that you aren't so clever after all. If you take up this challenge—and sometimes you'll feel like it—you won't be doing magic. You'll be engaging in a battle of wits with a spectator who is out to get you. And you might turn out to be the loser.

That brings us back to misdirection. As you know, misdirection often involves directing the attention of the audience away from the modus operandi of the effect and onto some unimportant detail the audience is convinced is important. In a repeated trick this is impossible, since the spectators now know what is and what isn't important. Imagine doing Passing Through with everyone watching the salt shaker instead of the coin. In a repeat performance, misdirection simply can't be as effective as it must be. The audience best prepared to see magic is an audience that doesn't know what's going to happen. Or, as Alkazar says in his *Red Notebook,* "He who knows not what to expect knows not what to suspect."

Now, there are certain effects that depend on repeated moves. *The Mirror,* which we will come to later, is one such effect. And so is the following effect, which Alkazar showed me not long ago, while we were hiking in the woods behind his studio. We'd been on the trail about an hour, when the wizard of wizards suddenly stopped and pointed to the ground.

"Look at those," he said eagerly. "Homing stones!"

"Homing stones?" I asked. "What are homing stones?"

"These are." Alkazar sat down on the ground and began sifting through a pile of small pebbles. "You've heard about homing pigeons and how they always return to the nest. Well, these are homing stones. I'll show you."

Alkazar smoothed out a little stage in the dirt and placed three of the pebbles in the center. "I'll put one of these stones in my left hand. And now a second one. But the third stone goes into my pocket. Now watch what happens—the lonely homing stone returns to the nest."

Alkazar opened his left fist and out rolled all three pebbles.

"Isn't it amazing?" the wizard went on. "I'll try it again."

Once more Alkazar placed two pebbles in his left hand and one in his pocket. He opened his fist, and out rolled all three. And while I was shaking my head in disbelief, he did it again.

"You know, you can't find these stones everywhere," Alkazar said, once more putting two stones in his left hand and one in his pocket. "Hmm. That's strange."

"What is?" I asked.

"How many stones would you say are in my left hand?"

"Three," I said, hoping to be a step ahead.

"That's what I would have thought. But look!" Alkazar opened his hand. All of the stones had disappeared. He reached into his pocket and took out all three stones. "I guess they found a new nest. Well, let's be off, shall we." And with that, Alkazar tossed the stones aside and headed down the path.

The secret of *Homing Stones* depends on a fourth stone about which the audience knows nothing, and a method of concealing that stone called *clipping*. There's no need to go out and hunt for stones or pebbles right now. This bit of magic can be done impromptu with all kinds of small, roundish objects such as beads, raw peas, or even spitballs. For close-up work, make a set of four balls by crumpling up 2-inch squares of aluminum foil. You can make larger or smaller balls later on, when you know what's most comfortable for you to hold in the clipped position.

Now, here's how to clip. Turn your right hand palm up and keep your forefinger and middle finger together. Take one of the balls and rest it on those fingers, on or slightly below the line of the top joints. With your right thumb, push down on the ball slightly and allow a bit of the ball to go between your fingers. Squeeze the fingers together lightly, remove your thumb, and the ball is now clipped in place. (See Figure 6-1.) Turn your right hand palm down, curl your fingers slightly, and relax your hand. Not only will the clipped ball stay in place, but no one will be able to see it.

Before you are ready to perform this effect, you must learn to use the clipping hand as if it were empty. With the clipped ball in place, practice picking up and putting down the other balls. To lift a second ball, simply place your fore- and middle fingers in front of it and your thumb behind it. Then squeeze and lift. (See Figure 6-2.) There's nothing difficult or unnatural about this, since it is most likely the way you would pick up the ball anyway. Keep the hand relaxed, with a minimum of pressure on the ball, and no one will ever be the wiser.

Now, let's imagine you've practiced for a while and are ready to go through the moves. I'm going to give them to you step by step, without patter, and you should try to follow them exactly.

Have the four balls or stones in your right pants or shirt pocket. Reach in with your right hand and clip one of the balls. Bring out the other three and drop them on the table. With your right hand, place the three balls in a line, a few inches apart. Now pick up one ball with your right hand and turn your left hand palm up. Place (don't drop) the ball on the left palm, move the right hand away, and close the left hand into a fist.

Next, pick up another ball. Open the left hand, revealing the ball inside, and place the second ball on the left palm. Just after your right fingers touch your left palm, begin to close your left hand as your right hand moves away. But instead of leaving only the second ball behind, leave it *and* the clipped ball. This means you now have three balls in your left hand, but the audience knows about only two of them. Now pick up the third ball—exactly the way you picked up the first two—and pretend to place it in your pocket. As your right hand goes into the pocket, roll the ball into the clip position and bring out your hand, relaxed and slightly curled, as if it were empty. During this move, keep your eyes on the other hand. Say a few words. Blow on your left hand if you like. Then open the hand and roll the three balls onto the table.

Now repeat the entire sequence of moves, exactly as described, and roll out the three balls. The fourth is again clipped in position. Go through the moves a third time, only this time leave the third ball in your pocket. Your right hand comes out empty, and the left reveals the three balls.

You are now ready for the final sequence in which the balls vanish and end up in your pocket. Pick up one ball and place it in your left hand exactly as before. Close the hand. Pick up another ball. Open the left hand to add the second ball and place it directly on top of the first, so that you can grip both balls. As the left hand closes, move the right hand away, carrying in it the two balls that are hidden in a stack behind the forefinger and middle finger and supported by the thumb. With the right hand, which never stops moving, pick up the third ball in the same manner and place it, plus the two hidden balls, in your pocket. (See Figure 6-3.) Remove your hand. The audience now believes that two balls are in the left hand and one in the pocket. Show that the balls have vanished. Reach into your pocket, remove three balls (leaving the extra behind), and roll them onto the table.

I leave it to you to develop this effect in any way you wish. It works well

53

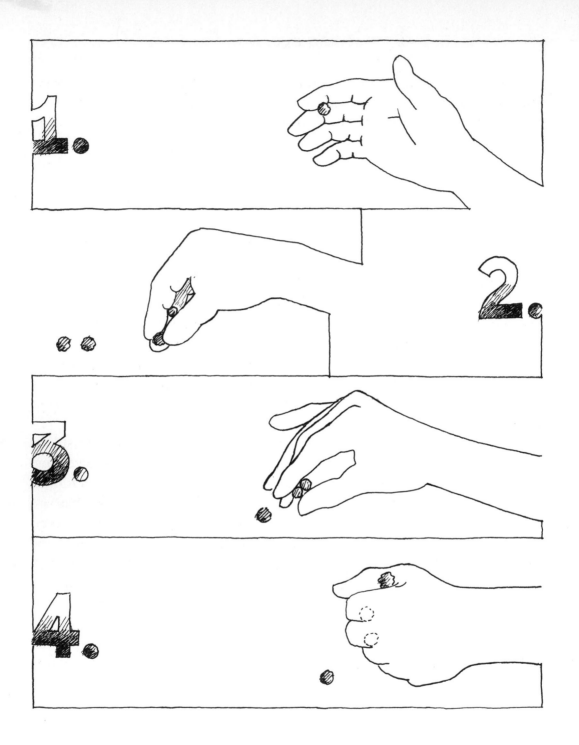

in this simple form, but a story could also be made up about the adventures of these three balls. For me, Homing Stones is one of the best impromptu tricks there is, and I have used it in many variations for years.

From the *Black Notebook:*

1. For its success, Homing Stones depends a great deal on boldness. You may at first be afraid of freely using the hand that hides the ball. But if you are overly cautious in your movements, you will call attention to them.

2. Never peek at the hand that hides the ball to see if it is showing. If you are not confident that the ball is hidden, you need more rehearsal.

3. When working impromptu with actual stones, clip the extra stone in the following manner: Sift through a pile of stones and remove seven or eight that are alike in size and color. Pick out the three you are going to use, and in getting rid of the others, secretly clip one. Since you haven't started the effect yet, no one will pay much attention to what you are doing.

4. Practice to get your timing perfect, especially when you add the clipped ball. You can expect to fumble for a while and have difficulty in releasing it. Keep at it. Don't be in such a hurry to close the left hand that you grab onto the fingers of the right. And never hesitate. Work for smoothness.

5. For variety, try this move on the second or third repeat. Instead of adding the clipped ball with the second ball, add it with the first. Then pick up the second ball from the table and place it on top of your left fist, which you turn so that the thumb is on top. (See Figure 6-4.) Pause. Then allow the ball to sink into your fist and join the other two. Put the third ball in your pocket and continue as before. This variation allows you to show your right hand as empty when picking up the second ball.

6. It is not necessary to have the balls end up in your pocket. You can simply conclude by having them disappear.

CARDS, PART ONE

magnetic touch

"Want to see a card trick, kiddo?" Alkazar asked, as I entered his studio for one of our weekly lessons.

"Sure," I said.

The renowned wizard took a deck of cards from his workbench and spread them face down in a fan. "Pick a card, any card. Remember it. Now put it back on top of the deck, face down."

Alkazar cut the deck twice, then turned the faces of the cards toward himself and began looking through the deck. "You don't think I can find it, do you?" he said. "But just watch. Lo and behold, here it is!" And he pulled out the ace of diamonds and held it before me. It was my card.

"Pretty great, huh?" he said. "Now let me show you a different one, even better. Here, pick a card, any card you want."

58

I took another, and Alkazar repeated the same trick he had just done. Only the card I had taken was different.

"Oh, what talent," the magician gloated. "And I've got plently more just as good. Want to see another?"

Before I could answer, Alkazar tossed the cards aside and broke into a broad grin.

"Forgive my little joke," he said. "You thought those tricks were the worst—and so did I. There wasn't anything magical about them and of course they were exactly the same."

That made me feel better. From Alkazar I always expected something wondrous.

"You do realize," my instructor went on, "that half the card tricks magicians do are the same trick I just showed you. But the good performer takes that silly little trick, dresses it up in some fancy clothes, and presents it as an object of beauty."

I was puzzled.

"Tell you what," said Alkazar. "Let's try an experiment. Go outside and then come back in, as if you'd just arrived for your lesson."

I returned to the room in less than a minute, but in that time, Alkazar had undergone a miraculous transformation. Suddenly there was a flash in his eyes and a grace to his hands that had not been there just a moment before. Alkazar the teacher was gone. This was Alkazar the magician.

"Do you realize," he greeted me, "how many millions of people play card games, yet know absolutely nothing about cards? For instance, did you know that a magnetic field exists between people and cards that draws certain cards to certain individuals? Haven't you ever played gin rummy or some other game and found the same card turning up in your hand again and again?"

I admitted that it had happened to me.

"That's the magnetic attraction," the wizard explained. "Most people are completely unaware of it. But it's quite real. I'll show you what I mean."

Stepping over to a small table, Alkazar brought out a deck of cards, had me shuffle it a few times, then held it in his left hand.

"I'm going to put the cards face down on the table, one at a time," he explained. "Neither of us will be able to see what they are. But any time you feel like it, I want you to say 'stop.' You may not realize it, but no matter when you stop me, it will be at that one card in fifty-two that is attracted to you at this very moment."

I let fifteen or twenty cards go by before I finally said, "Stop."

"Now, with both hands, pick up the card so that I can't see it, and remember what it is."

As I looked at the card, Alkazar began dealing more cards onto the table and told me to add mine to the pile whenever I wanted. When I did, he placed the rest of the cards on top of mine. He had me cut the deck a few times so that neither of us could know the position of my card.

"What I intend to do," announced my teacher, rubbing his fingertips together, "is find your card by sensing in it the same vibrations that attracted you to it. At no time will I look at the face of a card until I have either declared it to be your card or eliminated it. Let's begin."

Alkazar lightly placed the fingertips of his right hand on the top card. "This is not your card," he announced, turning it over and starting a face-up pile next to the rest of the deck.

"This isn't it, either," he continued, feeling the back of the next card and turning it over. "Nor is this, nor this, nor this."

After turning over more than a dozen cards, the master magician touched the back of the next card and immediately pulled back his hand, as if the deck had suddenly become scorching hot.

"Yes," he said, "there are some very strong vibrations here." He carefully touched the card again, but only for an instant. "No doubt about it," he concluded. "This is your card. Please name it."

60

"The nine of spades," I said.

"Please turn the card over. I don't want to touch it again, but it's perfectly safe for you."

I turned the card over. It was the nine of spades!

I was astounded. It seemed that it would take years of practice to be able to find a card just by touching its back. I asked Alkazar to teach me the secret.

"A nifty trick," the wizard agreed. "But suppose I teach you that pick-a-card trick I showed you first. It's the same as this one, you know."

"What do you mean?" I objected. "It's not the same at all. And besides, you said you didn't like that trick."

"I don't," said Alkazar. "But the tricks are basically the same. In the first one you took a card, put it back, and I found it. That's just what we did in this one."

"But the first time, you had to look at the cards," I said. "Now you did it by touching them."

"I did it how?"

"By touching the cards."

Alkazar nodded gravely and pulled at his chin. "My dear boy," he said, putting his arm around my shoulder, "I did just what magicians are supposed to do. I fooled you. The truth is, nobody can tell one card from another by touching it. Not even me."

"But what about the vibrations? What about my special card?"

"Misdirection and fairy tales. I made it all up to throw you off the track—and also to disguise the fact that I was doing the very same three-step trick I first showed you. That was the point of this experiment. Look."

Alkazar brought out a note pad. On the left side he listed the three steps of the card trick as he had first performed it. On the right side he described the same three steps, but as they had been elaborately disguised. The chart looked like this:

MAGNETIC TOUCH

THE BASIC VERSION

1. Pick a Card

The magician holds out a deck of cards and says, "Pick a card, any card."

2. Put It Back

The magician has the spectator place his card on top of the deck and then cuts the cards.

3. Find It

The magician looks through the cards, picks out the spectator's card, and shows it to him.

THE DISGUISED VERSION

1. Pick a Card

The magician talks about card games and magnetic vibrations and claims that certain cards are attracted to certain people at certain times.

The magician begins by dropping cards on the table and asks the spectator to say "stop" whenever he feels like it.

The magician tells the spectator that he has stopped at his "special card" and has him look at it in a special way.

2. Put It Back

The magician continues to deal cards into a pile and requests the spectator to replace his card whenever he wants to.

The magician then drops the rest of the cards on top and has the spectator cut the cards once or twice.

3. Find It

The magician places the deck face down on the table. He rubs his fingertips together in order to make them "more sensitive."

The magician touches the cards one by one until he feels a shock.

The magician asks the spectator to name his card. The magician asks the spectator to turn over the card the magician has indicated. It is the spectator's card.

62

"The same trick," Alkazar went on. "On the left side terribly dull, on the right side a near miracle. Change the way you do each of those three steps, and you can have a repertoire of card magic that is absolutely astonishing."

It all seemed fascinating and very ingenious to me. But as long and as carefully as I studied the list, there was one thing I couldn't figure out.

"How," I asked, "do you find the card?"

"Oh, that." Alkazar beamed. "That's the easy part. The difficult task is to master the themes that other magicians have created for us, and to create new disguises and invent new themes. That's where the imagination and creativity come in. Finding the card, that's child's play."

Alkazar leafed through the pages of his *Black Notebook* and quickly found what he was looking for.

"Some notes I've made," he said, handing me the book. "Copy this down, take it home, study it, and next week show me ten different ways of having a card selected—and I don't mean 'Pick a card, any card.'"

"But, Alkazar," I complained, "I still won't know how to find it."

"Trust me. If I told you how to find the card, you'd be terribly disappointed. The secret is so simple, so obvious, so easy that anyone half as smart as you could learn it in a minute."

"But I've got a minute," I said. "I have a whole hour."

"Then use it to copy my notes," said my teacher. "And besides, don't you think there's something delicious and wonderful about not knowing a secret? After all, it's an experience we magicians give our audiences all the time. I don't think you should miss it."

"But, Alkazar," I pleaded.

"I have spoken," he said. "Good-bye. And don't forget to practice."

After copying Alkazar's notes, I left the studio feeling deeply disappointed. I had had my weekly lesson and I hadn't learned one new trick. It wasn't until several weeks later that I finally realized just how much I had learned.

This is what I copied from the *Black Notebook:*

Basic card magic begins with the selection of a card, and ends with its discovery by the magician. The method of card selection is often unrelated to how the card is later found. Therefore, emphasis on the method of card selection constitutes misdirection.

Repeated use of the same method of card selection is boring. Varied methods of card selection encourage varied presentations. Some methods of card selection are better for some tricks than for others.

Fifteen Methods of Card Selection

1. Fan the deck in your hands and have one card removed.
2. Have the spectator cut the cards and remove the card he has cut to.
3. Have the spectator name a number. Count cards from the top of the deck and give the spectator the card at his number.
4. Have the spectator think of a number. Allow him to count to that number and take the card.
5. Spread the cards in a line or a semicircle and have the spectator remove one.
6. Spread the cards in a line or semicircle and tell the spectator to move his index finger back and forth along the row until he feels "an impulse" to stop. Have him remove the card he's pointing to.
7. Fan the cards behind your back and have one selected.
8. Tell the spectator to think of a card. Have him form a picture of it in his mind. Hand him the deck and tell him to remove the card he thought of.
9. Drop the cards one by one onto a table and have the spectator stop you whenever he feels the urge.
10. Riffle the edge of the deck with your thumb, and have the spectator stop you by inserting his finger in the deck and taking the card under it.
11. Make any number of piles on the table and have the spectator choose the top or bottom card of any pile.

12. Fan the cards and have the spectator choose a group of ten or twelve cards. Let him shuffle these and choose one.

13. Have the spectator deal cards face down until he feels he has come to a special card. Have him remove and keep that card.

14. Fan the cards so that the spectator can see the faces. Ask him to find one he really likes and remove it.

15. Have the spectator think of black or red. Then have him think of a suit of that color, and finally, a card in that suit. Hand him the deck and let him remove that card.

8

CARDS, PART TWO

super ears

As usual, the maestro was correct. How you actually find the card is often the easiest and least important part of card magic. What really matters, and what makes the strongest impression on an audience, is how it appears you find the card.

Nevertheless, every magician needs at least one undetectable method for finding a selected card. The system Alkazar first taught me is one of the oldest and best. It's called the *key card* method of card location. It is wonderfully simple to do, and impossible to detect when done properly. With it, you can produce some of the most baffling effects ever done with cards. Get a deck and you'll see how it's done.

First, look at and remember the bottom card of the pack. This will be your key card. Later it will show you the exact location of the *chosen card*—the one selected by the spectator.

Remove another card from the deck and pretend it is the spectator's card. Place the rest of the deck face down on the table and place the spectator's card face down on top of the deck. Now cut the cards and place the bottom half on top. Square the deck so that you can't tell where the cut was. Repeat this procedure twice more. The chosen card is now lost somewhere in the deck and no one—not even you—knows exactly where it is. But that doesn't mean you can't find it. Actually, the chosen card isn't really lost at all. It only appears to be. With that first seemingly innocent cut of the cards, you automatically placed the key card—the one that you know—directly on top of the chosen card. And it's still there.

If you had shuffled the deck, the key would probably have become separated from the chosen card. That's why you don't shuffle. Instead, you make the audience think the cards are thoroughly mixed by cutting the deck several times.

Most people have no idea that cutting the cards doesn't change their order at all. No matter how many times the deck is cut, the key will always be directly on top of the chosen card, provided the deck is reassembled—the bottom half put on top—after each cut.

To find the chosen card, simply turn the deck toward you, and look through the cards until you see the key. The card right in front of it, the one closest to you, is the chosen card. Or try this: Instead of looking at the cards, hold the deck face down in your left hand and begin turning cards face up, one at a time, placing them on the table. Watch for the key card. As soon as you turn it over, stop. The very next face-down card is the chosen card.

Simple, isn't it? But what do you do now? Remove the chosen card and show it to the spectator?

Never. One of the most elementary rules of pick-a-card magic is that you must disguise what you are really doing so that the discovery of the chosen card appears to be the result of some other process altogether. Alkazar's Magnetic Touch is nothing more than an excellent disguise for a simple key-card location. In that cloak, the magician appears to discover the chosen card by using his extraordinary sense of touch. But what he is actually doing—as he touches the cards and turns them over one by one—is watching for the key card to appear. When it does, the magician automatically knows that the next face-down card is the chosen one. He touches it—and the rest is acting.

On rare occasions, the spectator's final cut may return the key to the bottom of the deck, leaving the chosen card on top. You will not realize this until you have turned up all the cards. At that point, offer an explanation for not finding the card. Then turn the deck face down and cut it, bringing the key and chosen card together. Start again.

Before I give you another key-card effect—and there are plenty of good ones, as you'll see later—here is the proper handling of the key-card method. Learn it exactly, thoroughly, and in all its variations, and you will be able to perform under what spectators consider the most difficult conditions of all: with a borrowed, shuffled deck of cards and no advance preparation whatsoever.

The first step is to spot the key card. This must be done as early as possible and always before the trick begins, never during. And it must always be done in a way that goes unnoticed by the audience. Let's see how.

Suppose you have agreed to perform and someone hands you a pack of cards. Remove them from the case, look through them briefly (a natural thing to do), shuffle a couple of times, and finally square up the deck. In squaring the deck, it is perfectly natural to look at the cards to make sure they're lined up. That's when you spot the key—while squaring the cards. (See Figure 8-1.) To the audience, the trick does not yet seem to have begun, so the casual glance you give the bottom card—or the whole deck, for that matter—goes completely unnoticed.

Once you have spotted the key, it is a good idea to place the deck face down on the table and pay no attention to it, as you make a few remarks about what you are going to do. This is an important pause, because it further separates the spotting of the key from the selecting of a card.

It is also possible to get a peek at the bottom card while a spectator is shuffling the deck. As soon as you catch a glimpse of it, you must get the spectator to stop shuffling so that the key doesn't get lost in the pack. Say something like "Fine. Now put the cards face down on the table." If you are firm, the spectator will do as you tell him and never suspect that half of your work is already done. If you fail to get a key card during a spectator shuffle, simply take the deck back, square it up on the table, and take your peek.

Now for the methods of key placement. So far I have mentioned only one. The spectator places his card on top of the deck and the deck is cut and reassembled. This is fine when performing a single effect, but in a series of card tricks it is essential to have different methods of key placement. This not only creates variety, it hides the fact that the same system is being used again and again. Here, from the *Black Notebook,* are six of Alkazar's favorite and most deceptive key moves.

The key is on the bottom of the deck, already sighted.

1. Begin dealing the cards, face down, one at a time onto the table, thus forming a pile. Invite the spectator to place his card on the pile whenever he likes. When he does, drop the rest of the deck on top of his card and the others and square up the cards. The key is in place.

2. Place the deck on the table. Cut off half the cards and place them on the table next to the bottom half. With the same hand pick up the bottom half and hold it above the original top half. Indicate to the spectator that he should replace his card in between the two halves. Drop the top half on the bottom, and the key is in place.

71

3. Have the spectator cut the deck into two piles. Have him place his card on the top half and complete the cut. The magician never touches the cards, and the key is in place.

4. Place the deck on the table. Divide the cards into five or six fairly even piles and remember which pile contains the key. Have the spectator place his card on top of any pile. Pick up the pile containing the key and drop it on the pile containing the chosen card. Tell the spectator to place any pile on top of that one. Replace another pile yourself, have the spectator do the next, and so forth until the deck is assembled. The key is in place. If the spectator immediately places his card on the pile containing the key, have him cut that pile and complete the cut. Then have him assemble the piles in any way he chooses. The magician never touches the cards, and the key is in place.

5. Drop piles of seven or eight cards on the table. Tell the spectator to say "stop." When he does, have him place his card on top of the tabled cards and drop the rest of the deck on top of those. The key is in place.

6. Do an overhand shuffle from your right hand to your left. (See Figure 8-2.) Midway through the deck, pause, and have the spectator place his card on top of those in your left hand. Drop the rest of the deck, as a block, on top of those. The key is in place.

Following the placement of the key card, it is a good idea to cut the deck once or twice, or to have a spectator do the cutting. As we have seen, this helps create the impression that the chosen card is hopelessly lost in the deck. But equally important in building this illusion is the magician's over-all manner and the way he physically handles the cards.

Generally, the less attention paid to the cards, the better. In placing the key over the chosen card (in methods 1, 2, and 5 especially) don't be so delicate or neat that you call attention to what you are doing. Instead, drop the key (and all the cards above it) onto the chosen card, or replace it with a little toss. By being a bit sloppy, you create the impression that you couldn't care less which cards go where. And if you don't seem to care, neither will the audience.

Practice different methods of key placement so that you can do them without thinking. Learn to spot and remember the key card at a glance. Never show any reaction when the key card turns up. Never appear to be remembering something. Never let uncertainty or hesitation show, unless it is part of the act. Master the key-card method and it will serve you well.

The following effect is a simple key-card discovery. It is based on a theme similar to Magnetic Touch, but with a couple of twists. See if you can figure it out.

SUPER EARS

The magician or a member of the audience shuffles a deck of cards and places them face down on the table. It is well known, the magician claims, that a person's voice changes whenever he tells a lie. True, many people are skilled liars and can get away with all kinds of fibs—but never in front of anyone who has developed "super ears."

To demonstrate his own super ears the magician has the spectator remove a card from the deck, show it to the others, and return it to the pack. The cards are cut a few times and held by the spectator. He is told to say, "None of these cards is my card," and to then turn over the cards one by one and name them. No matter how hard he tries to disguise his voice, or keep it exactly the same, the magician claims he will know when the spectator names his card. And to make certain he doesn't get any clues from the spectator's face, the magician turns his back and walks several feet away.

73

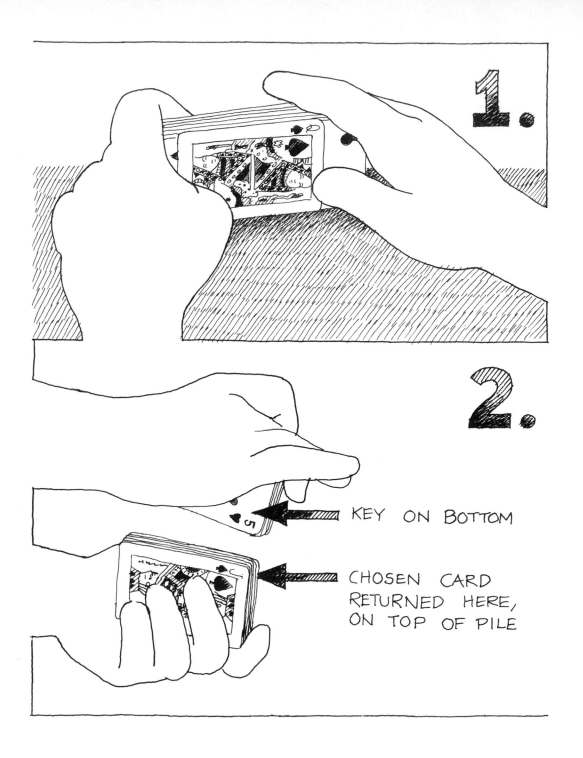

1.

2.

KEY ON BOTTOM

CHOSEN CARD
RETURNED HERE,
ON TOP OF PILE

One by one, the spectator calls out the names of the cards. Twice the magician stops him and asks him to repeat a card he has just named.

"No, that's not it," says the magician. "Please continue."

After several more cards have been named, the spectator is stopped again and asked to repeat the last turned-over card. "No, that's not it, either," says the magician. "Name the one before it. Please say, 'That's not my card.'"

The spectator complies, at which point the magician counters, "You're lying—that is your card."

And of course it is.

CHAPTER
9
CARDS, PART THREE

the speller

the assistant

the mirror

esp

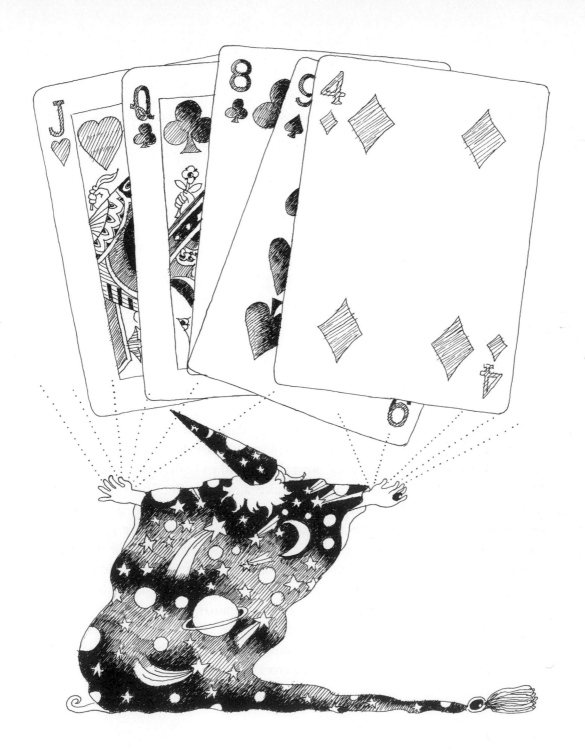

Now that you know the secret of the key card, you are ready to master a beautiful array of card magic. All the tricks that follow are the basic three-step trick Alkazar first taught me, and all depend in some way on a key card. Magnetic Touch and Super Ears are quite alike in effect and only slightly different in method. In Super Ears, which you may have figured out by now, the magician listens for the key card instead of looking for it. When he "hears" it, he remembers the next card (the chosen card) but allows the spectator to call one or two more cards before stopping him. He then asks the spectator to back up and name the previous two cards before finally singling out the chosen one. This backing up adds greatly to the dramatic effect of the trick. Other variations on the same theme include pretending to find the card by taking someone's pulse, looking into his eyes, or holding his hand, all the while turning cards over one by one.

By working out new themes and presentations for the discovery of a card (and using the secret of the key), you'll be well on your way to inventing some fine, original card magic. But before you tackle that project, try mastering the next four tricks. They are clothed in some of the most ingenious disguises magicians have ever sewn together for key-card use. And with them, you'll create miracles.

THE SPELLER

The effect is this: The spectator chooses a card, shows it to the rest of the audience, and returns it to the deck. The magician looks through the deck but is unable to find the card. He gives the cards to the spectator and asks him to spell out the name of the chosen card, turning over one card at a time for every letter in the name. When the spelling is completed, the next card on the deck is turned face up. It is the chosen card.

Here's the method.

As always, begin by spotting the key. Have a card selected (methods 1, 2, 5, 7, and 14 all work well) and returned to the deck in order to get the key on top of it. Have the deck cut once or twice.

With the faces of the cards toward you, look through the deck as if searching for the chosen card. When you see the key, remember the name of the chosen card (right in front of the key). Beginning with the key card, silently spell the name of the chosen card while transferring one card from the left hand to the right for every letter you spell. For example, if the chosen card is the eight of clubs, spell *e-i-g-h-t-o-f-c-l-u-b-s* and transfer one card at a time for each letter. (See Figure 9-1.) As soon as this is completed, stop, but don't lose your place. Look directly at the spectator and tell him you can't find his card. At the same time, move your hands apart, taking the cards you spelled and those with them in your right hand and keeping the rest of the pack in your left.

Immediately say to the spectator, "But I've got a better idea. Here. You take the cards." As you say this, put the cards back together—but reverse the order of the two halves so that the right-hand cards end up as the new top portion of the deck. Immediately hand the cards to the spectator.

The deck is now set up for the dramatic conclusion. Ask the spectator to name his card and then tell him to spell it aloud, turning over one card for every letter. Don't forget the *o-f.* When the spelling is complete, pause for a moment of suspense. Then have the spectator turn over the very next card. To everyone's surprise but the magician's, it is the chosen card.

Occasionally, when the chosen card and the key end up near the top of the deck, you may run out of cards before you complete your silent spelling. For example, say you spell *j-a-c-k-o-f-c-l-,* when you reach the top of the deck and are out of cards. Simply square up the pack and continue from the bottom of the deck. The first three cards you shift from your left hand to your right will be the *u-b-s* you need to complete the spelling. Now move your hands apart, claim you can't find the card, reverse the halves (in this case one "half" has only three cards) and give the deck to the spectator. This trick is a gem.

THE ASSISTANT

The performer explains that magicians often use secret helpers to accomplish their magic. These assistants open trap doors, work hidden threads, and do all manner of unseen and unappreciated work. In fact, they even help out in card tricks. The magician offers to demonstrate.

A card is chosen and returned to the deck. The magician admits that he has no idea what the card is. But fortunately his assistant, a fellow named Jack, has been following things very closely. Jack does know what the card is. The performer removes the jack of spades from the deck and introduces it as his secret assistant. He says a few words to Jack, holds the card to his ear, and apparently hears it reply.

1.

A KEY CARD, START SPELLING HERE
B CHOSEN CARD
C SEPARATE DECK HERE AND REVERSE HALVES

SPECTATOR'S SIDE

KEY ON
BOTTOM

CHOSEN CARD GOES
FROM CENTER OF
DECK TO ORIGINAL
TOP

PERFORMER'S SIDE

2.

"Tell me," says the performer to Jack, "what was the name of the card? . . . What do you mean, you want a day off! You just had one. Now tell me the name of the card. . . . A ten, did you say? Well, which ten? . . . Not a ten? . . . What do you mean, you're not telling unless you can have next Tuesday off?"

Things go in this way until finally the magician gets the information he wants.

"I'm not sure I can believe this guy," he says, "but according to Jack you took the two of hearts. Is that right?"

And of course it is. End of trick.

The key card is again the real assistant in this trick. After it is in place over the selected card and the deck has been cut a few times, the magician picks up the deck and removes the jack. It is while looking for the jack that he secretly spots the key and learns the name of the chosen card. After the jack is removed, the remainder of the deck is tossed aside. The rest depends on a good script and good acting.

In an alternate version, remove Jack from the deck and introduce him to the spectators before you have a card selected. Have the chosen card returned to the deck and get the key on top in the usual manner. Then return Jack to the deck and instruct him to get the information you need. Make a few cuts, remove Jack, and the rest you know.

THE MIRROR

This next effect requires two decks of cards, one for the spectator and one for the magician. It is a classic of card magic. Its traditional name is *Do As I Do,* but Alkazar, for reasons you'll soon see, has given it a different title. Like many card effects, it is best done while the magician is seated at a table.

"Mirrors have always fascinated me," Alkazar begins. "I've spent hours studying them and staring into them, and I've made quite a few remarkable discoveries. Perhaps the most fascinating is my discovery that mirrors not only reflect events in the real world, they can also cause them. Let me show you what I mean."

Alkazar gives the spectator one deck of cards and keeps the other for himself.

"Shuffle your deck until you're satisfied that all the cards are well mixed, and I'll do the same with mine."

After shuffling, the magician and the spectator exchange decks so that each has the pack shuffled by the other.

"What I'd like you to do," explains Alkazar, "is play the part of my reflection. Everything I do, you do. I'll do everything slowly so that we can stay close together. Agreed? Good. Let's begin by putting our cards on the table."

The decks are placed face down on the table opposite each other.

"I'm going to push my deck forward about two inches," Alkazar explains, "and you do the same with yours. Now I'm going to cut off about half my deck, and you do the same."

Alkazar cuts off the top half of his deck and puts it on the table to the right of the bottom half. The spectator does the same, but he places his top portion to the left of his pack so that it is opposite Alkazar's.

"Now let's each remove the card we cut to. You remember yours and I'll remember mine. Now let's put the cards back and complete the cut."

When this is done, Alkazar has the deck cut two more times, each time insisting that the spectator follow his moves exactly.

"Now," says Alkazar, "let's exchange decks again. From your pack I'm going to take out the card I peeked at and put it face down on the table. You do the same thing from the deck you now have."

The two cards are laid opposite each other on the table.

"Now, as I turn mine over, you turn yours over."

The two cards are turned over simultaneously. They are identical! What's more, Alkazar then repeats the procedure two more times, and each time the cards match—like reflections in a mirror.

As you will discover when you master The Mirror, there is something extraordinary about the reaction this effect produces in audiences. Although it's nothing more than the same old three-step card trick, it appears to audiences to be totally unique. It is one of the great ones.

Now, here's how it's done. After you and the spectator have shuffled your decks, spot and remember the bottom card of your deck. Then exchange decks, and the key card will be on the bottom of the spectator's deck.

The decks are now cut and a card is removed from the middle of each deck. Tell the spectator to remember his card and you will remember yours. Peek at your card, making sure no one else sees it, but don't bother to remember it. As you will see, it plays no part in the trick.

Next, return your card to what was the top of your deck and have the spectator do the same with his card. (See Figure 9-2.) Complete the cuts. The key card is now in place over the spectator's chosen card.

After one or two more cuts, exchange decks with the spectator. Look through the deck you now hold and pretend to remove the card you peeked at. Actually remove the spectator's chosen card, which is right next to the key. Place this card face down on the table, preferably before the spectator does so with his. The two cards are turned over. They are, of course, identical.

This procedure is so subtle it can be repeated two or three times without fear of detection.

ESP

Like The Mirror, this effect is so neatly disguised that it can be presented not as card magic but as something else entirely: a demonstration of mind reading. Here is Alkazar's presentation.

The subject of mental telepathy is being discussed, and the performer offers to demonstrate his sensitivity to the "thought waves" of others.

Alkazar approaches a member of the audience who, he claims, appears to be a suitable subject for the experiment.

"Right now," says the magician, "I want you to think the word *stop*. Don't say anything, don't do anything, just think *stop*."

Alkazar looks the spectator directly in the eyes.

"Please think it louder, as if you were shouting. In fact, scream the word *stop*—but only in your mind."

After a moment, the magician appears to have actually heard the spectator's word. "You'll do fine," he says. "Come. Please help me with this."

Alkazar has the spectator choose any card in the deck, remember it, and put it back. The deck is cut once or twice, and the magician begins to deal cards one at a time, face up on the table.

"When you see your card, say nothing. But think the word *stop* as loudly as you can."

After a few cards are turned up, Alkazar explains that his concentration is being broken by seeing the cards. He hands the deck to the spectator, turns his back, and shuts his eyes.

"Just keep dealing the cards," Alkazar instructs. "When you see your card keep on dealing, but think *stop*."

The spectator may deal a few cards or many. But sometime while he is dealing, Alkazar suddenly commands him to stop.

"I think I heard you. But please don't say anything, just think! That last card you dealt, was that your card? Just think, was that your card, yes or no? No? Okay, the card before it? Just think, was that your card, yes or no? Yes? Okay, that was your card. Am I correct?"

The spectator, if he can speak at all after this astounding demonstration, admits that it was his card.

Remember, the magician does not see the cards as they are being dealt, nor does the spectator say anything. The magician can be several feet away from the proceedings and can even be blindfolded. Yet he always gets the card. How?

The answer is the "delayed key," a system in which the key card is placed a certain number of cards away from the chosen card. It doesn't matter how many cards away, as long as the magician knows.

To produce the effect of ESP, spot the bottom card on the deck and remember it as your key. Next, drop cards from the top of the deck onto the table one by one. As you do this, silently count the number of cards you drop. Tell the spectator to stop you at any time. (This is method 9 of card selection, with the counting thrown in.) When the spectator stops you, have him look at and remember the last card you dropped. Let's assume it was card number 10. Remember this number.

While the spectator is looking at his card and showing it to others, drop the rest of the deck onto the pile on the table and square up the pack. Now have the spectator return his card to the deck by key placement method 5 (others work as well), and have the deck cut once or twice.

Start to deal the cards face up on the table one at a time, as you instruct the spectator to think *stop* when he sees his card. Keep dealing until you deal the key. At this point, stop and complain about your difficulties in concentrating. Give the cards to the spectator, turn your back, and tell him to continue dealing slowly.

What you now do actually requires concentration. You might ask for silence from the audience so that you may "focus your mind." You'll need the silence because what you're doing is secretly counting the cards as you hear them being turned over and placed on the table. When you get to the number you remember, 10 in our example, you will know that the chosen card is lying face up on the table. As in Super Ears, it is good showmanship to let the spectator deal another card before you stop him. Then backtrack and identify the chosen card.

You will learn as you continue your study of magic that the use of a key card is not the only way a magician can keep track of a chosen card. Nor is locating a chosen card the only thing a skilled card worker can do. Yet with these two devices and your imagination, you can create a variety of astonishing effects.

In several cases, I have left it up to you to choose the methods of card selection and key placement for the effects in this chapter. And the themes offered, detailed as some may seem, are really only outlines for performances that you must construct on your own.

In doing so, try not to base your magic around the finding of a selected card. That gets very boring. But mind reading, mysterious coincidences, an unexplained phenomenon, the magician's sense of touch—these are the things that turn tricks into magic.

10

NATURALNESS

coins through the table

"Do it right under their noses," shrieked the maestro. "And relax! You act like you're hiding something in your hand."

"But I am," I said.

"Of course you are. But that doesn't mean you have to act like it. Why, a cactus could see what you're doing."

We were working on *Coins Through the Table,* one of the great illusions of close-up magic, in which four coins apparently penetrate a solid tabletop. I'd been rehearsing for nearly a month, but there were still flaws in my performance.

"It's better," Alkazar admitted, "but it still doesn't look natural. You're holding your hand too stiffly. And stop rushing. You're working too fast. A perfectly natural appearance, that's what we're after. Now start again, from the beginning."

90

As Alkazar taught me, a natural appearance is one of the most difficult things for a magician to achieve. Acting "naturally" simply means doing something the way we ordinarily would—directly, easily, and without thinking about it. But, unlike naturalness in daily life, which happens automatically, a natural appearance in magic is often contrived to cover something going on secretly. And, far from happening on its own, it is the result of a great deal of study and practice.

The supreme importance of a natural appearance is that it is rarely questioned. Unusual or unfamiliar actions cause people to wonder what's going on. Natural and familiar actions cause people to assume they know what's going on. In Coins Through, for example, there is a key move in which the magician must secretly lap a coin and, at the same time, convince the spectators that he has picked up that coin and moved it from one hand to the other. If there is anything at all unusual about the way this deception is carried out, the audience will spot it easily. On the other hand, if everything the magician does seems relaxed and natural, just as it would appear if he were really moving a coin, the spectators will not only pay little attention to the move, they will automatically accept that a coin is now in the other hand. It is not necessary for the spectators actually to see the coin to be convinced that it is there. The naturalness of the magician's behavior will cause them to assume it.

The best way to develop a natural appearance is to observe and then learn to imitate perfectly the ordinary way of doing something. But this is not as easy as it sounds. The "natural way" of performing even the most simple task can never be pinned down to a single action. Rather, naturalness is a pattern of behavior, a combination of many actions that together create an overall impression of familiar movement. You must ask, for example, how fast does someone ordinarily move when reaching for a coin? Where does he look? Is his head tilted or straight? Does he pause before completing the action? If so, when? For what reason?

It can take weeks of practice to coordinate the timing of patter, body movement, pauses, and gestures into what must finally be a smooth and flowing whole. But it will be worth all the time and effort. As Alkazar said, "A natural appearance is like a curtain of ordinariness behind which the magician can hide the very essence of his craft. It is his invisible cloak—and one of the essentials of great magic."

The basic effect of Coins Through is that, one by one, four coins are passed through a solid tabletop. The instructions are elaborate but not hard to follow if you take the time to understand each step before going on to the next.

Begin by sitting at a table, keeping your midsection a few inches from the edge. Keep your knees, which are under the table, pressed together. Imagine that there are spectators seated around the other sides of the table. Bring out four coins, quarters or half dollars, and drop them on the table near the center. Adjust your chair, pull up your sleeves, or otherwise indicate you are ready to begin.

THE FIRST COIN

Call attention to the coins. Pick up one coin with your left hand and place it on your right palm in the position shown in Figure 10-1. Add the other coins, one at a time, counting aloud as each coin is placed on the right palm. Extend your hand forward (it is a few inches above the tabletop) and show the coins. Now, turn your hand counterclockwise and drop the four coins into your cupped left hand, forming a fist around them. Or rather, make the audience think that's what you've done.

Actually, only three coins are dropped into the left hand. By slightly curling the third and fourth fingers of your right hand as you rotate that hand, you can keep the first coin you picked up secretly in place between the base of the fingers and the middle joints. This is called a *finger palm*. Keep the back of the hand toward the audience, with the fingers loose and slightly curled, and the coin won't show. (See Figure 10-2.)

Immediately after transferring the coins, move your closed left hand forward to a position a few inches above the center of the table. At the same time, lower your right arm so that your hand comes to rest near the edge of the table in front of you. Remember, the right hand is supposed to be empty after the transfer of the coins, so it is natural to get it out of the way by resting it near the table's edge. (See Figure 10-3.) Both hands should reach their destination at the same time. Relax your right hand, maintain the natural curl, and allow the finger-palmed coin to fall into your lap.

During this sequence, keep your eyes focused on your left hand. When you have lapped the coin, look at a spectator and explain that you are going to cause one of the coins to pass through the table. Keep your left hand still. Choose the exact spot (which we'll now refer to as "the spot") where the coin will penetrate, about 1½ feet in front of you, and with your right hand, point to or touch the spot. Allow your audience to see that your right hand is empty. This will strengthen the spectators' assumption that the left hand contains four coins. Now, without comment, turn your right hand palm up, show it, and place it, palm up, under the table directly below the spot. This will cause you to lean slightly forward. Then, secretly bend your right arm at the elbow, find the coin on your lap, and bring it back to a position under the spot. Look at the spectators, then at the spot. Then slap your left hand on the table, opening it directly on the spot. Press down as if pushing one of the coins through. Pretend to feel it go. Act pleased. Bring up your right hand and show that one coin has penetrated. At the same time, casually lift your left hand and show that only three coins remain. Place the coin that's in your right hand on the table to your right. Look at the audience and pause for a moment as if the trick were over.

THE SECOND COIN

Three coins are in a group near the center of the table; the fourth coin is on the table to your right, about 3 inches from the edge. Without saying anything, pick up one of the three coins in the following manner. Place the fingertips of your right hand on top of the coin so that it is completely covered, and slide it along the table toward you. When you reach the edge of the table, place your right thumb underneath the coin to keep it from falling. Lift the coin, place it in your palm-up left hand, and close the hand over it. The sliding and the lifting of the coin are one continuous motion, with no pause or hesitation when you reach the edge of the table.

Immediately reach for another coin from the center and pick it up in exactly the same way. Open your left hand and toss the second coin in so that it lands on top of the first and makes a clinking sound. Close your left hand.

Bring the third coin toward you, using the same sliding motion as before. Only this time when the coin reaches the edge of the table, allow it to fall into your lap. Don't try to flick the coin toward you, simply let it fall. Without hesitating, continue the motion of picking up the coin by placing your thumb under the imaginary coin and lifting it. When your right hand reaches the position in Figure 10-4, look directly at someone in the audience and say, "Watch, I'll do it again." On "watch," your right hand is motionless, as if holding the coin. On "I'll do it again," simultaneously open your left hand and "add" the imaginary coin from your right. As you do, strike the two coins in the left hand with the thumb or fingertips of your right hand so that the coins clink. This contributes to the illusion that the third coin has been added. Close the left hand into a fist.

The moving of the "three" coins from the table to the left hand should happen in an easy rhythm, one after another, and should take about 3 or 4 seconds. Remember, each of the coins is slid off the table and picked up in exactly the same way. The coin is always hidden behind the fingertips and does not show, whether it is actually there or not. The displaying of the imaginary coin on "watch" is a bold move. However, it would be the natural thing to do if you had a coin, so doing it helps create the illusion that you have one. Believe it, and the audience will, too.

When the third coin has been "added," extend your left hand forward and shift your gaze to the remaining coin on your right. Pick it up with the identical sliding motion and display it on the right fingertips. Look at the audience as if you had nothing in the world to hide.

As before, place your right hand, with its single coin, under the table. Secretly pick up the lapped coin, and move your hand under the spot. Hold your left fist a few inches above the spot. Look at the audience, then at the spot. Slap the left-hand coins onto the table. Push, act pleased, and bring up the right hand, revealing the two coins. Casually lift your left hand, showing that only two coins remain. Leave these on the center of the table, and place the two coins in your right hand on the table to your right. Pause.

THE THIRD COIN

Look at one of the spectators and say, "Let's try it again." As you say this, pick up one of the center coins, using the sliding motion described before. Hold your left hand open, palm up, about 2 inches above the table so that the fingers are above the table but the heel of the hand extends beyond the edge. Place the coin openly in the finger-palm position on the left hand and keep the hand open. Pick up the second center coin, using the sliding motion, and place it on the left palm slightly below the center of the palm. Look at the two coins and say, "These two stay above." Close your hand.

With your right hand, pick up the two remaining coins, one at a time, displaying them on the open right palm, and say, "These two go below."

While performing the action with the right hand, lap one of the coins in the left hand in the following manner. As you pick up the coins with the right hand, turn the left hand slightly clockwise so that the thumb is on top. Lower the hand to the table so that it comes to rest with the knuckle and part of the little finger on the table, and with the heel of the hand beyond the edge. (See Figure 10-5.) Since all of the work is presumably being done by the right hand, the relaxing and lowering of the left will seem to be a natural movement. After the left fist contacts the table, relax the fingers, and, without losing the illusion of a tight fist, allow one of the coins to fall

95

into your lap. Release the coin while you are in the process of looking at, picking up, and displaying the right-hand coins.

After saying "below," keep both hands motionless for a second, the closed left hand resting on the table and the right with coins displayed on the fingertips. Then move both hands at the same time. Move the left forward over the spot and the right, with the coins, under the table. Secretly pick up the lapped coin. Look at the audience, look at the spot, then slap the third coin through. Bring up the three coins from below and place them on the table to your right, as you lift your left hand to reveal the single coin in the center.

THE FOURTH COIN

The final coin, like the second, is lapped while you are apparently picking it up. The sliding motion has now been legitimately used enough since coin two to arouse no suspicion. It may therefore be done slowly, deliberately, and with complete confidence.

Begin by placing the fingertips of your right hand on top of the coin and sliding it toward you. Naturally, you must look at the coin when you reach for it, but while sliding and apparently picking it up, look directly at a spectator and say, "The last one is always the hardest." By the time you say "hardest," your right hand has completed the pickup motion (the coin is on your lap) and is held perfectly still for a second, as in Figure 10-4. This freeze in motion only lasts a second, but it strongly establishes the impression that your hand holds a coin. Again, displaying the coin would be the natural thing to do. Therefore, appearing to display it "proves" to the audience that the coin is there.

Follow the action with your eyes as you pretend to place the coin in your left hand and close your fingers around it. Immediately move your right hand, and your gaze, to the three coins. Pick them up one by one with the sliding motion and display them. Keep your left hand still and away from the edge of the table. Look directly at one of the spectators, as if to say, "Okay, everything is fair and square. Now watch."

Simultaneously, move your left hand over the spot and place your right, with the coins, under the table. Pick up the lapped coin in the usual way, only this time grip it between your thumb and fingers in preparation for some final misdirection. At the exact moment your left hand slaps its imaginary coin onto the table, slap the right-hand coin loudly against the underside of the table. The audience will assume the sound they hear comes from the left-hand coin. (Eliminate this move when working on a tablecloth.) Push down with the left hand and allow the single coin to drop into the right, where it joins the rest of the coins with a clink. Act pleased at your success. Bring up your right hand, and drop the four coins onto the table as you lift your left hand to show that the final coin has passed through.

Coins Through should be practiced from 15 to 20 minutes a day. Once you have the general idea, develop the naturalness of each deception by alternating it with the genuine movement. With your right hand, slide a coin toward you from the center of the table, pick it up, place it in your left hand, and close your fingers around it. Now repeat the same movement, but this time lap the coin and only pretend to pick it up and place it in your other hand.

Go back and forth between the two movements and try to make the false pickup look exactly like the genuine version. Pay particular attention to where you look, the speed of your movements, the natural timing of pauses, and the manner in which you use your hands and fingers. All the details of the real action belong in the sleight.

Once you have gone through this process for each deception, work on the entire routine in the same way. Learn everything as described, before adjusting any part to your personal style. All the deceptions and all the movements leading up to and following them must be above suspicion.

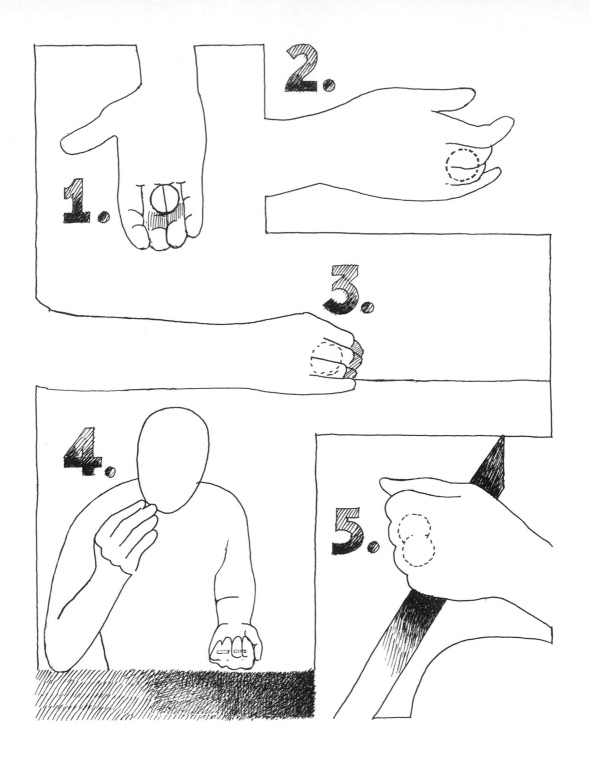

Three themes from the *Black Notebook:*

1. Science has shown that nothing is really solid. Passing matter through matter is accomplished by merely striking at the right time.

2. Spells may be conjured into existence through magical drawings and symbols. Using his finger as a pencil, the magician sketches an invisible geometric pattern on the table. Coins placed in the center of the drawing pass magically through the table.

3. The magician asks to borrow "a hole." Since no one present has one, the magician brings out one of his own. The hole is invisible, since it is made "entirely of nothing." The magician places the hole on the table and demonstrates its existence by passing coins through the hole and the table. Upon concluding, the magician neatly folds the hole and replaces it in his pocket, or awards it to a spectator.

From the *Red Notebook:*

1. Everything the audience sees the magician do must seem logical and ordinary.

2. The magician must always act naturally, according to his own character or the character he is playing.

3. When the natural results in the impossible, magic is achieved.

11

ROUTINING

card in orange

In order to create the most entertaining magic shows, it is important to temporarily put aside your desires as a performer and become, instead, a director. Magicians are notorious for performing too long and specializing in the effects they like best. It is up to the director to curb the magician's self-interest and do only what is best for the audience and for the show as a whole.

The effects you select for a particular program will, of course, be strongly influenced by the age of the audience and the performing setting—close-up, living room, or stage. But a successful magic show often depends not so much on the choice of tricks, but on how well the director has coordinated them into a total performance. Alkazar has done a lot of thinking on this subject, and I have copied down some of his best ideas from the *Red Notebook*. These rules apply to magic in all settings and for all audiences, and I urge you to study them carefully.

ALKAZAR'S PRINCIPLES OF ROUTINING

1. *Open with impact.* Make a strong first impression on the audience. When possible, begin with a trick that is short, friendly, and contains a surprise. "Look," the opener should say, "there's magic here!"

2. *Keep the show moving.* Allow the audience to experience the full astonishment of each effect, but introduce your next trick before they've quite finished reacting to the last. This not only unifies the show, it also denies the audience the opportunity to try to figure out how the previous effect was created.

3. *Change the pace.* As in a guided tour, there are certain places where the sightseers must be allowed to linger in order to take their fill of the local wonders. Other attractions need only a quick stop to be fully appreciated. Construct your shows so that they have both long and short effects, brisk and leisurely pacing.

4. *Vary the effect.* If something disappears in one trick, don't make anything disappear in the next. When you use elaborate equipment in one trick, use little equipment in the following. Mix dramatic presentations with light-hearted ones, complexity with simplicity, audience participation with a solo number. Even specialized routines—card magic, for example—require a good mixture of effects.

5. *Keep it short.* Lest the audience get tired or bored, keep the show short. A close-up act can last from 10 to 20 minutes, a living-room show from 20 to 35. A stage show can last as long as 40 minutes. When sharing the bill with other performers, 10 to 15 minutes is enough. Short shows are better.

6. *Stop.* Always leave the audience wanting more. Encores are acceptable only if planned. Close your routine with an effect that always gets an enthusiastic response. Let the audience enjoy their response, and end the show. The only way to leave them wanting more is to stop. Never do "just one more."

With these rules in mind, let's put together a sample routine. Below are all the available effects, including two you have yet to learn.

Close-up Show	*Living-room Show*	*Stage Show*
Sweet Deception	The Cords of Shastri	The Stamp Collector
Passing Through	Cut and Restored Rope	The Cords of Shastri
Magnetic Touch	The Stamp Collector	Card in Orange
Super Ears	The Assistant	The Spirit of Isis
Cut and Restored Rope	ESP	
The Speller	Card in Orange	
The Mirror		
The Assistant		
Homing Stones		
Coins Through the Table		

Since your most common performing opportunity will be for close-up work, let's try putting together a close-up show for a small group of adults or people your own age. It should be done with everyone, including the magician, seated around a table. For an opening trick, my choice would be Passing Through. It captures the audience's attention, makes them doubt the magician's powers, and then hits them with a strong surprise that leaves them startled and eager for more.

104

Once the audience is hooked, it might be a good idea to slow things down and present a more elaborate, dramatic effect. How about Magnetic Touch? It gives the audience a chance to participate in the routine, offers a different category of effect, and provides a slow and deliberate pace that's a nice change from Passing Through. Furthermore, it is easy to get into. Just as the spectators are beginning to recover from the previous effect, all you need do is bring out a deck of cards, turn to someone and ask, "Do you play cards?" No matter what the response, move directly into Magnetic Touch, allowing no conversation on Passing Through. Build Magnetic Touch to its exciting conclusion, and reveal the card.

Cut and Restored Rope follows well, but my own preference is for The Assistant. A pair of card effects that seem totally different from each other makes a nice interlude in a close-up show. Furthermore, The Assistant lightens the serious tone of Magnetic Touch and, again, the transition between the two effects is easily made. As the spectators express their astonishment at your miraculous sense of touch, begin to gather the cards and say (possibly in response to a spectator's comment), "Well, I have to admit I had a little inside help. Actually, I have an assistant, a fellow named Jack. . . ." And you're into The Assistant.

To close this show, I like Homing Stones. It does not require audience participation, as the card effects did, so all attention is once again focused on the performer. Also, it is different from anything performed so far. As a transition from The Assistant, you can have Jack request his favorite trick, or you can simply bring out the stones and say, "There's one more thing I want to show you before I stop." It is a good idea to warn the audience that the end of the show is near; this prevents them from anticipating more and feeling disappointed at not getting it.

The complete act, then, consists of Passing Through, Magnetic Touch, The Assistant, and Homing Stones. A routine just as good, though slightly longer, is Homing Stones, Super Ears, The Speller, Sweet Deception, and Coins Through the Table.

The rest of the routining duties I leave to you. By using the fifteen tricks in this book in various combinations, you should be able to create a couple of medium-size or living-room routines, a stage show, and a number of specialized routines as well. There's a great "psychic powers" act to be made from The Mirror, Sweet Deception, and ESP, and a nice cards-only routine with Super Ears, The Speller, The Assistant, The Mirror, and ESP. Just make sure you adhere to Alkazar's principles and use some common sense about the choice of effects and themes. Children enjoy flashy equipment, interesting stories, and lots of audience participation, while adults are more easily entertained by the performer's skill and the cleverness of the effects.

Once you have a complete act, write down the sequence of tricks on an index card, along with all the props you need. Keep it visible during a performance until you know the routine by heart. Over a period of time, observe what kind of reaction individual tricks get from an audience. Effects that evoke a positive response belong in the routine. Those that don't—no matter how much you like them—should be pulled, and other effects should be substituted. When a routine is finalized, do it until it becomes second nature. And when someone asks you to perform, don't respond with "some tricks," but rather with a total performance that will make your reputation as a truly exceptional magician.

I have chosen *Card in Orange* for this chapter because it is one of the few effects that can fit into almost any routine. It is a card mystery, a disappearance, a reappearance, and a restoration act all in one. And it is one of the most perplexing and entertaining feats ever invented. There are many presentations possible (I've included two from the *Black Notebook*), but the basic effect, without frills, goes like this:

A card is chosen by a volunteer and torn into several pieces. The volunteer retains a corner of the card, and the remaining pieces are placed in a paper cone, from which they quickly disappear. The missing card is then discovered inside an orange that has been in the possession of another volunteer from the very beginning of the trick. The card is completely restored except for the missing corner, which is still held by the first volunteer. The corner matches the card perfectly, proving that only one card has been used.

To perform this effect, you'll need a large orange, two decks of cards with identical backs, a vanishing cone like the one used in The Stamp Collector, and a method of forcing the "right" card on the volunteer. Let's start with the cards.

Decide which card will be used—let's say it's the queen of hearts—and place it on top of one of the decks. Put the cards back in the card case (with the queen on top) and put them aside until show time. Remove the queen of hearts from the second deck and get rid of the rest of the cards, as they play no part in the trick. Tear off the upper left-hand corner of the duplicate queen and place the piece in the secret compartment of the vanishing cone. (See Figure 11-1.) Put the rest of the card aside for a moment.

From a large orange, remove and save the pip (the part where the stem was attached). Starting at that spot, poke a deep hole through the center of the orange. A pencil will do the job nicely, but take care not to let the point come out the other side. (See Figure 11-2.) Now take the duplicate queen (the one with the missing corner), roll it into a tight cylinder, and insert it into the center of the orange. If the card proves too long, fold over one third before inserting. (See Figure 11-3.) Use the eraser end of the pencil to poke the card well into the orange. Glue the pip back in place so that the orange looks exactly as it did before you started any of this. To prevent the card from becoming soggy, make these preparations as close as possible to show time. When the glue dries, you're all set.

To perform, have two volunteers come forward to assist you. Remove the prepared orange from a bowl containing other fruit and give it to one of the assistants. Remove the cards from their case, approach the second volunteer, and briefly fan the deck to show that all the cards are different.

Make sure the top card is not exposed as you open and close the fan. If you are working standing up, place the deck, face down, on your left hand. Extend that hand toward the volunteer and ask him to remove about half of the cards. Take the remaining cards in your right hand and have the volunteer place his cards on your left palm, which is now empty. Place your cards crosswise on top of the spectator's, so that the point at which the cards were cut remains clear.

Now you must shift the audience's attention. Holding your left hand stationary, turn to the first assistant and make some comment about the orange. Ask a question or exchange a few remarks. Then return to the cards, and with your right hand lift off the crosswise portion and extend the remainder of the deck (on your left hand) toward the volunteer. Thumb the top card toward the spectator and say, "Take a card, please. It doesn't matter if I see it."

Because their attention has been distracted, neither the volunteer nor the audience will realize that the selected card didn't come from the center of the deck, as it appears, but is actually the original top card, the queen of hearts. This deception is called a *cut force*. (To do it seated, place the cards on the table. Have the volunteer cut the deck and place the bottom half on top, crosswise. Distract the volunteer for a few moments, then lift the cut.)

After the selected card has been shown to the audience, have the volunteer tear the card in half across its width, place the top two pieces on top of each other, tear across the width again, and then once more. While this is being done, bring on the vanishing cone. Take the pieces of the card from the spectator, and place them in the secret compartment of the cone. At the same time, remove the corner already in the cone and hand it to the volunteer as if you were returning one of the pieces just given you. "Why don't you hold on to one of these" is the attitude.

To complete the effect, vanish the pieces from the cone, or make them fly invisibly into the orange. Retrieve the orange from the assistant, and with a sharp knife, cut through it until you reach the card. Then rotate the orange and finish cutting around but not through the card. Now comes the climax that will have the audience delirious. Twist the orange halves in opposite directions, separate the halves, and display the rolled-up card in the center. (See Figure 11-4.) This is an awe-inspiring sight, so give the spectators a moment to realize what they are seeing. Then unroll the card, take the corner from the spectator, and show that the two are a perfect match.

Here are two presentations from the *Black Notebook:*

1. One spectator holds a rope and an orange. The second spectator selects a card and tears it into pieces. All the pieces but one are placed in a paper cone. The performer holds one end of the rope against the orange. The magician sends the torn card through the rope and into the orange. The missing piece proves it's the same card.

2. This comedy version of Card in Orange gains its humor by contrasting the magician's bravado and overconfident manner with his inability to make anything go right. It stands by itself as a complete 5-minute stage act.

The performer summons two volunteers from the audience and positions them on opposite sides of the stage. He attempts to vanish an orange directly from the hands of one volunteer. Failing, he approaches the second volunteer—leaving the first with instructions to hold the orange at arm's length—and has a card selected and returned to the deck. Despite his claims as a superior card technician, he fails to find the card and asks the spectator to retrieve it from the deck. As the spectator looks through the cards, the performer races to the other side of the stage, where he again fails to vanish the orange and ends up leaving it covered with a handkerchief.

Returning to the card trick, the performer has the original chosen card torn into pieces. He places the pieces in a paper cone—"unwittingly"

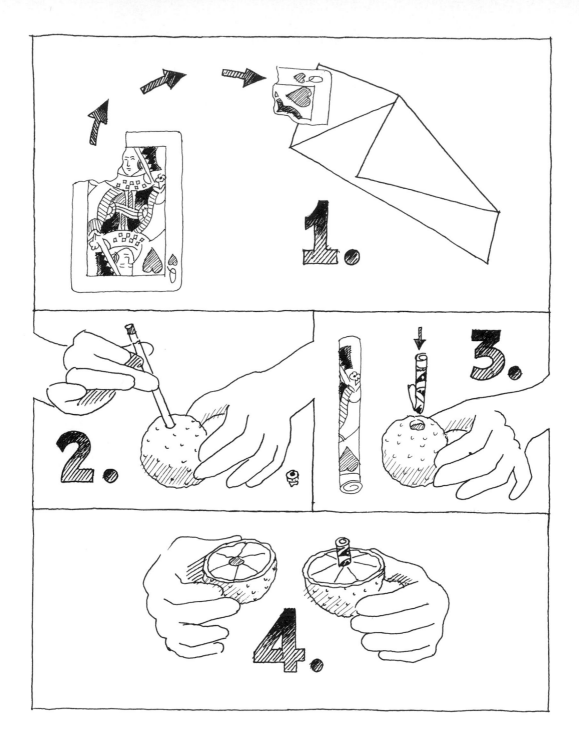

dropping a single piece to the floor—and claims he will restore the card to its previous condition. Instead, the card disappears, leaving the magician thoroughly perplexed. He notices the piece on the floor and gives it to the spectator to hold until the rest of the card turns up. He races across the stage and whisks the handkerchief from the orange. Frustrated by its refusal to disappear, the performer declares that the orange is faulty. He cuts it open and, to his own amazement, discovers the card. Even more amazing, the corner proves a perfect fit.

12

PERFORMANCE

the spirit of isis

It is time for the finale to your performance. As you approach the foot-
lights, you trace an invisible circle in the air with your hand and instantly
the lights dim. The stage is bathed in a soft blue glow and distant music is
heard. The audience is suddenly quiet.

With the aid of the assembled guests, you explain, you are about to attempt a spiritual contact with the goddess Isis, one of the most powerful
magicians in Egyptian myth. In order to do so, you must enter a deep
trance. In fact, you tell the audience, you have already begun to bring on
this hypnotic state, which may take possession of you at any moment.
When it does, you will be unaware of everything around you and will be
cared for by your trusted assistants, who have more than once helped you

pass through the dangerous portals of the netherworld. The two assistants, dressed in Egyptian costume, have come onstage and are quietly working behind you. They clear an area in the center of the stage, and on a low stool or altar, they place a lighted candle.

To evoke the proper atmosphere, you ask the audience to imagine they are inside an ancient Egyptian tomb deep within one of the great pyramids. You describe the scene, the paintings on the stone walls, the casks of glittering jewels, the mummies. Then, suddenly, you stop speaking. A shudder seems to pass through your body. The trance is taking possession of you. You place your hands, palms together, in front of your chest and breathe deeply several times. Your eyes close, your breathing seems to stop, and you are motionless.

Your assistants have been watching attentively, and now they quickly bring forward a large bolt of cloth and wind it around you, mummy-style, so that you are covered from head to toe. They move your rigid body to the center of the stage and place you behind the altar. As the music grows louder, your assistants chant an ancient spell and pass their hands up and down before your body. A shimmering gong is heard, signaling the completion of the spell. Your helpers quickly unwind the cloth—but you are gone! In your place, in full Egyptian costume, is the goddess Isis! Slowly she raises her hand and points toward the rear of the auditorium. The audience turns just in time to see you come racing down the center aisle. You leap onto the stage, take Isis by the hand, and together bow to the audience, as your show comes to a dramatic end.

The Spirit of Isis is one of the finest and most dramatic stage illusions that can be presented without expensive equipment. The secret is simple: As the trick begins, Isis, a third assistant, is hidden offstage in the wings. As the assistants raise the cloth to wrap the magician, they temporarily screen the space between the performer and the wings, allowing the magician and Isis to change places without being seen. It is a bold move that requires split-second timing and absolute coordination among the magician, Isis, and the assistants.

To begin: Isis is waiting offstage in the left wings. (See Figure 12-1.) You complete the previous effect, then walk downstage center (or downstage right) and, in your most serious manner, begin some carefully planned patter about ancient Egypt, mummies, the flight of souls through space, and the hypnotic trance that will soon take possession of you.

While you are setting the mood and hinting at what is to come, you are deliberately positioning yourself at the exact point on the stage where the switch will take place, namely, downstage left, parallel to, but about 2 feet to the right of, the left wings. (See Figure 12-1.) You could simply walk to this area to begin with, but you don't want the audience to suspect there's something important about this particular spot. You have explained that you may go into a trance at any moment, and this provides you with a logical reason for stopping anywhere, anytime you want. In short, you move from stage right to stage left, pattering about ancient Egypt, when suddenly you stop (you've just hit the spot) and enter the trance.

Meanwhile, the assistants have been quietly working in an area just upstage of center. They have moved aside any equipment and set up the "altar" (a decorated orange crate will do). On the altar they have placed a candle and perhaps even some incense, which one assistant has lighted. The second assistant has brought out a large cloth (an Indian bedspread, or a double sheet, dyed or spray-painted) and has begun to unfold it.

It is important that the assistants finish their preparations just as you are entering your trance. They observe what is happening and allow your trance to deepen. As your breathing seems to stop, they look at each other, then move toward you. One assistant carries the partially unfolded cloth draped over his arm.

From here on, the timing must be perfect. Assistant *A* crosses in front of you and stands to your left. Assistant *B* stands to your right with the cloth. Together they unfold the fabric between them, stretch it taut, and raise their hands above their heads so that the cloth hangs from their fingertips to the stage floor, completely hiding you from the audience's view. As the cloth is brought into this position, assistant *A* should be slightly downstage of the entrance to the wings and far enough stage left so that the outstretched cloth momentarily screens the space between you and the wings. At the exact moment this position is reached, change places with Isis. (See Figure 12-2.)

What I have described in steps must actually be done as one continuous action if the switch is to be totally invisible. The assistants do not open the cloth and then get into their proper places. Correct positioning must happen as a result of unfolding and stretching the cloth. The exchange of the magician with Isis must be so smooth and quick that the audience is aware of not a second's hesitation between the stretching of the cloth and the mummy-style wrapping. And—amazing, but true—if the magician and Isis change places simultaneously, the area between the performer and the wings need not be screened for more than two seconds at most!

The moment you are offstage, head for an exit and work your way to the back of the auditorium. Meanwhile, the assistants wrap Isis in the following manner. Assistant *B* places his end of the cloth against Isis's back and holds it in place at arm's length. At the same time, *A* begins winding the cloth around Isis in a counterclockwise direction. (See Figure 12-3.) This "catches" the cloth against Isis's back and allows *B* to let go and get out of the way.

A continues winding the cloth around Isis as many times as it will go, while *B* helps by adjusting the cloth and making sure the wrapped figure is completely covered at all times. Isis should have her palms together in front of her chest, just as the magician did, to help disguise differences in build. Although the wrapping process may sound complicated, a few rehearsals will show you how easy it is.

Once Isis is completely wrapped, the assistants tilt her slightly backward, and, supporting her from the back and under the elbows, pull her to a position in the center of the stage behind the altar. Remember, the audience still believes that the wrapped figure is the magician in a deep hypnotic trance. Behind the altar, Isis is stood upright, and the assistants make a variety of magical passes around her. All this should allow you plenty of time to get to the back of the auditorium. When you are in place, the assistants sound a gong (or give some other indication that the climax of the trick is at hand). Then Isis is unwrapped and you return gloriously to the stage.

The Spirit of Isis is an illusion that will accommodate all the showmanship and inventiveness you can cram into it. In first describing the trick, I mentioned the use of Egyptian costumes, lighting changes, and mysterious music. These are all additions to the basic effect that will make it splashy and colorful, if that's the direction you want your magic to take. But such additions involve more rehearsal time and more assistants than you may have, and more problems than you may want. A splendid illusion can easily be created without them. In fact, you may want to take the opposite approach and limit your presentation to just a few props, a bare stage, the three assistants, and yourself. That, too, is showmanship.

From the *Black Notebook:*

1. Always use an "Isis" who is about the same height and build as you are.

2. Make sure the wrapping cloth is heavy enough that it cannot be seen through when stretched taut. If the light source comes from the front this will present no problem. Also, make sure the cloth is trimmed so that no more than 4 or 5 inches of cloth gather on the floor when the assistants hold it above their heads.

3. You may have to leave the building to get to the rear of the auditorium from backstage. Always check out exits and entrances to make sure they won't be locked during a performance.

4. Arrange to rehearse on the stage where you will perform.

118

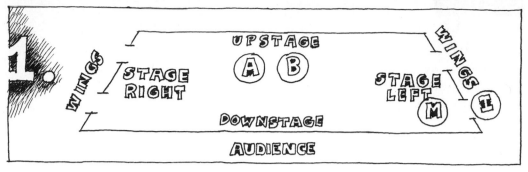

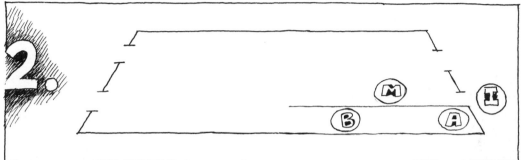

5. Check the time it takes to get around the theater, and make sure your assistants have enough to do to fill the time.

6. Have a fellow magician or trusted friend attend a rehearsal and tell you how it looks from the audience.

7. Work on the switch until the timing is perfect. And don't settle for anything less.

8. *An alternate performance:* "The Magician Masked." An assistant appears in costume, wearing a mask that completely covers his face. This figure, with the aid of a second assistant, hypnotizes and helps wrap the magician. The second assistant moves the magician to centerstage, while the masked assistant brings a lighted candle from the wings and places it on the altar. The masked figure makes magical passes in front of the magician and removes the cloth. The magician is gone, and someone else is in his place. The masked figure now removes his mask and costume. It is the magician.

Two identical sets of masks and costumes are needed. The masked assistant "hypnotizes" the magician. The magician changes places with the third assistant in the usual manner. Offstage, the magician immediately puts on the duplicate costume and mask. While one assistant moves the wrapped figure to centerstage, the masked assistant goes offstage for the candle. The magician in duplicate costume returns with the candle and places it on the altar.

The discovery that the figure who hypnotized and helped wrap the magician *is* the magician is absolutely stunning.

Afterword

It is Alkazar's belief, and it has become mine, that a magician's apprenticeship must be devoted to mastering the fundamental principles on which effective magic is built. All have been discussed in this book. However, there are several hundred deceptive moves, formulas, principles, and devices that have gone unmentioned here. Of course, no gimmick or secret is worth very much unless the performer also possesses the ability to transform it into magic. But now that you have that ability, you are ready to learn more.

Other books are perhaps the best place to begin. The public library should have at least a few of the dozens of magic books written for beginners. When you are ready for more sophisticated tricks, you might consult the technical and highly specialized books and pamphlets written especially for magicians. These are available only at magic stores.

If the yellow pages of the phone book reveal a nearby magic store, it's certainly worth a visit, not only to purchase books or tricks, but also to meet other magicians and learn about any magicians' clubs or organizations that might be in your area. Magicians are a friendly clan, and magic stores are usually eager to welcome beginners, or any potential customers.

But the best way to learn more magic would be from a good teacher. They're not hard to find. Alkazar never advertised for his students, yet those of us who cared enough somehow managed to find him. Perhaps you will, too.